11/08

DATE DUE

DISCARD

FIRE and EXPLOSIVES

FORENSIC EVIDENCE

FIRE and EXPLOSIVES

JOHN D. WRIGHT

SERIES CONSULTANT: RONALD L. SINGER, M.S.
PRESIDENT, INTERNATIONAL ASSOCIATION OF FORENSIC SCIENCES

Sharpe Focus
an imprint of M.E. Sharpe, Inc.

First edition for the United States, its territories and dependencies,
Canada, Mexico, and Australia, published in 2008 by M.E. Sharpe, Inc.

Sharpe Focus
An imprint of M.E. Sharpe, Inc.
80 Business Park Drive
Armonk, NY 10504

www.mesharpe.com

ISBN: 978-0-7656-8117-1

Library of Congress Cataloging-in-Publication Data

Wright, John D., 1938-
  Fire and explosives / John D. Wright.
    p. cm. -- (Forensic evidence)
  Includes bibliographical references and index.
  ISBN 978-0-7656-8117-1 (hardcover : alk. paper)
  1. Fire investigation--Juvenile literature. 2. Explosives--Juvenile
literature. 3. Chemistry, Forensic--Juvenile literature. I. Title.

TH9180.W75 2008
363.25'964--dc22
                              2007006750

Editorial and design by Amber Books Ltd
Project Editor: Michael Spilling
Copy Editor: Brian Burns
Picture Research: Kate Green
Design: Richard Mason

Cover Design: Jesse Sanchez, M.E. Sharpe, Inc.

Printed in Malaysia

9 8 7 6 5 4 3 2 1

PICTURE CREDITS

Ahura Corporation: 74
Corbis: 16 (Leif Skoogfors), 24 (Brian Snyder), 27 (Brian Snyder),
    31 (Tom & Dee Ann McCarthy), 32 (Michael S. Yamashita), 38 (Butch Dill),
    42 (Bill Stormont), 46 (Jonathan Blair), 54 (Bettmann), 57 (Bojan Brecelj),
    62 (Ron Sachs), 63 (Gilles Fonlupt), 67 (John Zich), 70 (Shannon Stapleton),
    72 (Bettmann), 75 (Simon Kwong), 85 (Bryn Colton), 86 (Andy Clark),
    88 (Ralf-Finn Hestoft), 90 (Kai Pfaffenbach)
Dreamstime: 20, 22
Getty Images: 10 (Hulton Archive), 14, 17 (Hulton Archive), 19 (Chuck Nacke),
    25 (Doug McFadd), 29 (David Drapkin), 30 (Robert Sullivan), 34 (David McNew),
    37 (Joe Raedle), 41 (Tom Cooper), 51 (Hulton Archive), 52 (Phil Degginger), 60, 64 (Alex Wong),
    69 (Jeff J Mitchell), 76 (Ali Al-Saadi), 79 (Ramzi Haidar), 80 (Paul K. Buck), 82 (Bob Daemmrich), 87
Photoshot: 7, 8 (UPPA), 12 (Noah Berger, UPPA), 48 (Stephen Dalton, NHPA)
Private Collection: 35, 55
Rex Features: 44
Topfoto: 58, 91

Contents

Introduction

As we approach the end of the first decade of the twenty-first century, interest in the forensic sciences continues to grow. The continued popularity of television shows such as *CSI*, *Crossing Jordan*, *Bones*, and the like has stimulated such an interest in forensic science among middle and high-school students that many schools now offer "forensic science" as a subject choice alongside the more traditional subjects of biology, chemistry, and physics. Each year, the number of colleges and universities offering majors in forensic science at both undergraduate and graduate level has increased, and more and more graduates are entering the job market looking for positions in the forensic science industry. The various disciplines that comprise forensic science provide the opportunity to use education and training in ways that the average student may imagine is rarely possible. On a day-to-day basis, the forensic scientist is called upon to apply the laws of science to the solution of problems that may link a particular individual to a particular crime scene or incident. Alternatively, the same tools and techniques may exonerate an innocent person who has been wrongly accused of committing a crime.

The four books that make up this series—*DNA and Body Evidence*, *Fingerprints and Impressions*, *Fire and Explosives*, and *Hair and Fibers*—are designed to introduce the reader to the various disciplines that comprise the forensic sciences. Each is devoted to a particular specialty, describing in depth the actual day-to-day activities of the expert. The volumes also describe the science behind those activities, and the education and training required to perform those duties successfully. Every aspect of forensic science and forensic investigation is covered, including DNA fingerprinting, crime scene investigation and procedure, detecting trace evidence, fingerprint analysis, shoe and boot prints, fabric prints, ear prints, blood sampling, arson investigation, explosives

High explosive is the most destructive type of explosive material. It normally needs a detonator, which sets off a smaller explosion, to work effectively.

analysis, laboratory testing, and the use of forensic evidence in the courtroom, to cover just a brief sample of what the four volumes of *Forensic Evidence* have to offer. Pull-out feature boxes focus on important aspects of forensic equipment, procedures, key facts, and important case studies.

Numerous criminal cases are described to demonstrate the uses and limits of forensic investigation, including such famous and landmark cases as the O.J. Simpson trial; cases of mistaken identity, such as Will West, who was at first confused with his identical twin and eventually cleared via fingerprint analysis; notorious serial killer Jack Unterweger, who was eventually convicted using DNA analysis from a single hair; and the work of the Innocence Project, which has used DNA analysis to retrospectively overturn wrongful convictions.

In *Fire and Explosives*, the author covers how fire and explosives work, what fires can reveal to investigators, famous arson cases, the history and uses of explosives, the methods by which forensic investigators detect and identify explosives after an explosion, and the use of explosives by terrorists. Written in a plain, accessible style, the series is aimed squarely at the general reader with an interest in forensic science and crime scene analysis, and does not assume previous knowledge of the subject. All technical language is either explained in the text, or covered in an easy-to-reference glossary on pages 92–93.

Taken as a whole, the *Forensic Evidence* series serves as a comprehensive resource in a highly readable format.

Ronald L. Singer, M.S.
President, International Association of Forensic Sciences

chapter 1

How Fire and Explosives Work

Fires and explosions are destructive entities that occur in different ways. They often become weapons used by arsonists and terrorists.

All fires and explosions are chemical reactions that need oxygen to ignite, but oxygen feeds them in different ways. Fire needs air around its flames, while an explosion draws oxygen from the materials used. This means fires can grow slowly, but explosions happen almost instantly. Knowledge of the workings and attributes of fire and explosives is essential for forensic scientists who deal in criminal cases involving **arson** and terrorist bombings. A successful investigation requires sharp skills to collect evidence left at the scene, identify it in a laboratory, trace it back to the seller or manufacturer, and make the final solid link to the criminal who purchased it.

Fire

Our atmosphere is about 21 percent oxygen, but a fire needs only 16 percent oxygen to burn. A fire heats up air, which rises

◁ **Fires can cause massive destruction in crowded metropolitan areas. Although modern fire departments have the latest equipment, some fires are too large to control.**

KEY FACTS **FIRES IN HISTORY**

Large tragic fires have started in many different ways. Some causes are uncertain; for example, there is the legend that Mrs. Patrick O'Leary's cow kicked over a lamp and started the great fire that burned much of Chicago in 1871. Others are obvious: San Francisco's famous 1906 earthquake caused a terrible fire that destroyed buildings left standing in its central district.

Accidents are a major cause. In 1942 at the Cocoanut Grove nightclub in Boston, a lit match ignited an artificial palm and drapery, killing 492—the deadliest nightclub fire in history. The entire building was engulfed in fifteen minutes. And in 1985, a stray lit cigarette supposedly began a fire on wooden seats at a soccer stadium in Bradford, England, killing fifty-six and injuring 260.

Fire investigators, however, have failed to solve some of the worst tragedies. A 1944 Ringling Brothers Circus fire in Hartford, Connecticut, took 167 lives, but authorities could never agree on whether the cause was a cigarette or an arsonist.

Numerous buildings in San Francisco burn following the terrible earthquake in the city in 1906.

and creates a **vacuum**. More air then rushes into that vacuum. A large blaze—for example, a wildfire—can pull in winds of up to 120 miles per hour (193 kilometers per hour).

The essentials needed to produce fire are heat, fuel, and oxygen, a combination often called the **fire triangle**. An increase in any of these intensifies a fire, while the absence of any one of them will put it out. A fire extinguisher might use carbon dioxide gas, which displaces the lighter oxygen around the burning object. Fire-retardant materials either have fillers such as **hydrated alumina** to release water at a high temperature, **halogenated compounds** to create a heavy gas that cuts off oxygen, or a protective insulating layer of **char** to keep out oxygen.

Many sources can produce heat, such as a match or other burning object, lightning, **friction**, or light focused through a glass. The fuel, also called the combustible material, is simply the object that catches fire, such as wood, paper, gasoline, or coal. A larger amount of fuel usually makes a fire hotter and helps it spread faster. Each type of fuel must be heated to its own ignition temperature to catch fire (*see* page 13, Key Facts: *Ignition Temperatures*). When wood is set on fire, for example, it might have to reach 617 degrees Fahrenheit (325 degrees Celsius) to burn, although this depends on the type of wood. Smaller objects take less heat to reach their ignition temperatures, so kindling wood burns quicker than a log.

When a flame first appears, a material has reached its flash point. This is the lowest temperature needed to form combustible gas to mix with air. If a material has a high flash point, there is less danger of it suddenly bursting into flames. The color of a flame is determined by what is burning and how hot it is. A flame's hottest part, usually its base, is blue and its cooler parts burn orange or yellow.

Flammable Material

A fire would appear very complicated if the chemical reactions of its atoms were visible to the eye. The most flammable materials contain carbon and hydrogen. Their atoms and those of oxygen react to heat by rapidly combining with other atoms or molecules. When a basic fuel like methane burns, more than 100 separate chemical reactions occur. This is a type of chain reaction that releases

energy as heat and light, which is the fire. What takes place within the flames is a result of matter changing form.

Surprisingly, what's seen burning is not the object, such as a log, but the gas it gives off after being heated. This gas rises just a bit to mix with oxygen and burns. Smoke is also a gas made up of oxygen, carbon, and hydrogen. As gas burns away, a log on fire breaks down into two leftovers: ash, made of minerals that do not burn; and char, which is mostly carbon. Charcoal is pure carbon. Some fuels—for example, gasoline—vaporize as a gas without leaving char.

An especially destructive type of fire in the United States and Canada is the

KEY FACTS **IGNITION TEMPERATURES**

If a material catches fire because of a spark—from a match, for example—it has a lower ignition temperature than if it caught fire by itself. Fire investigators speak of "piloted" fires, which are fires we light, and "unpiloted" ones, which are spontaneous. The list below shows some unpiloted ignition temperatures. Note how much more heat is needed for wood to burn in an unpiloted fire than a piloted one (*see* figure mentioned on page 11).

Fuel	(Fahrenheit)	(Centigrade)
Acetone	869°	465°
Butane	788°	420°
Corn oil	740°	393°
Gasoline	536°	280°
Hydrogen	952°	500°
Olive oil	650°	343°
Sulfur	450°	232°
Wood	1110°	600°

◁ **A firefighter tackles a wildfire in Colorado. A wildfire can rage through an immense area, consuming hundreds of thousands of acres and covering several counties of a state.**

wildfire. These infernos burn some 5 million acres (2 million hectares) in the United States each year. They are often started by campfires, cigarettes, normal trash burning, lightning, and even arsonists.

Feeding off trees, underbrush, and fields, a wildfire can travel more than 14 miles per hour (22.5 kilometers per hour), consuming homes and anything else in its path. Combustible material around a fire is called its **fuel load**, which becomes a tinderbox when dried out by the heat of the approaching fire. An intense fire can transfer heat to ignite bordering areas even before the wildfire arrives. Wind is a main factor, giving a fire more oxygen and determining its direction. Fires also create their own intense winds, which sometimes become **fire whirls** that twist like a tornado and toss flaming pieces in all directions.

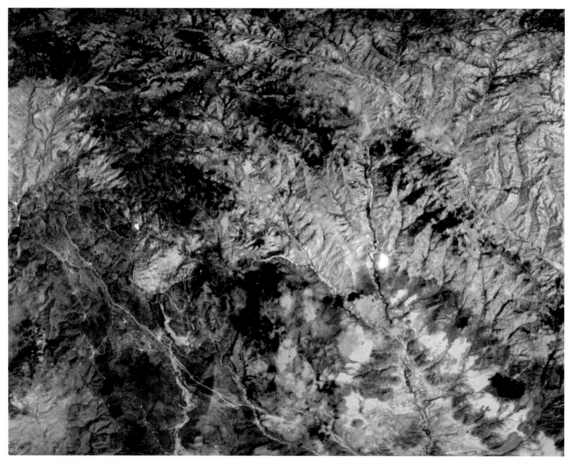

This NASA image of Arizona's Rodeo-Chediski wildfire on July 1, 2002, shows burned areas in yellow and brown and active fires in bright yellow.

Like any fire, however, a wildfire ends when its fire triangle is broken. The heat can be reduced by rain or by firefighters using water and fire retardants. The fuel can run out, often because firefighters create a **firebreak** with trenches, clearings, or even "backfires," which they set deliberately to burn away fuel in the wildfire's path. (The latter is also sometimes used to prevent a wildfire before it exists: firefighters set a controlled "prescribed burn" to reduce a region's available fuel.)

Like all fire investigators, those who deal with wildfires are patient and diligent in finding evidence. During one blaze in 2006 near Lake Arrowhead, California, the veteran fire investigator Brad Burns guarded the fire's point of origin all day until the spot cooled. He then joined other investigators on their hands and knees to sift through piles of blackened **chaparral** and trees for evidence. The seat of the fire had to be guarded, he noted, because firefighters fighting a blaze may accidentally douse the area with water or foam and contaminate the evidence.

Explosions

Explosions mostly detonate rather than catch on fire. When an explosive chemical compound or mixture detonates, it releases heat and gases that expand rapidly to produce energy in the form of pressure, or a shock wave.

The most destructive materials are called high explosives. They detonate almost instantaneously with a powerful blast effect. Examples are bombs and other large weapons. This outward blast can reach nearly 30,000 feet per second (9,150 meters per second), and within milliseconds the temperature can exceed 3600°F (2000°C). Explosives used in grenades and shells are called **brisant** *(bree-sawn)* **explosives**, and are able to shatter things.

This type of explosion builds up pressure so quickly that it creates a shock wave. One of the explosives with a high brisance is cyclotrimethylene trinitramine *(cyclo-try-meth-e-lean try-night-ra-mean)*—RDX for short, and also known as cyclonite. The best-known explosive materials include: **nitroglycerine** *(nite-row-gliss-er-in)*, dynamite, trinitrotoluene *(try-night-row-tol-u-ene)*—TNT for short; RDX (cyclonite); and **ammonium nitrate**. Two materials used in recent terrorist attacks are the organic peroxide **TATP** and the liquid explosive **Astrolite G**.

High explosives often have a blast sequence consisting of a small primary charge called a **detonator** that sets off a secondary charge referred to as a booster. Its shock then detonates the large main charge, which is called a bursting charge or burster charge. Mercury fulminate, an explosive salt, is an example of a detonator; TNT can be used as a booster; and RDX is a popular bursting charge.

Anyone handling a high explosive should be aware of its level of danger. Nitroglycerine is so unstable and sensitive it is normally mixed with an inert chemical to make it less explosive if jarred. TNT, by contrast, is highly resistant to shock and friction, and is therefore comparatively safe to handle. Some explosives are toxic, such as RDX and picric acid, which is structurally similar to TNT. The danger comes from improper handling, as when dust is inhaled or powder comes into contact with the skin.

Nuclear explosions are in a league of their own. The powerful energy of a nuclear blast comes from fusion or fission *(fisshin)*. Fusion, as seen in a hydrogen bomb, occurs when lighter elements melt to form heavier ones, with the difference in mass creating the destructive energy. Fission, as seen in an atomic bomb, occurs when neutrons split the **nuclei** of a heavy chemical element, such as uranium or plutonium, in a very rapid chain reaction. Both fission and fusion produce heat many millions of times greater than normal

A Bosnian Serb soldier shows an antipersonnel mine to NATO soldiers. Nicknamed "Bouncing Betty," the weapon pops into the air to explode and kill people within a 50-foot (15-meter) radius.

A mushroom cloud rises ominously over the Pacific Ocean on May 15, 1957, when Britain tested its first H-bomb near Christmas Island.

chemical processes, so nuclear weapons are tremendously more destructive than any normal explosion. The atomic bomb dropped on Hiroshima in World War II had the blasting power of 25 million pounds (11 million kilograms) of TNT.

Low explosives are used as **propellants**. They are said to "deflagrate" rather than detonate, which means they burn rapidly with intense heat and sparks but do not normally make a large explosion. They produce a **subsonic** explosion of less than 3,300 feet per second (1,007 meters per second). A low explosive is used to propel a bullet in a gun, because it gives a relatively slow push inside the barrel without exploding and damaging the weapon. However, low explosives are used to shatter weaker weapons, such as a pipe bomb or Molotov (mol-o-tov) cocktail, which is a bottle filled with gasoline.

Black powder, called **gunpowder**, was the most common propellant for hundreds of years. It was made by mixing solid **oxidizers** and fuels. It was dangerous and produced a lot of smoke, but is still used for **pyrotechnics**, such as fireworks and signaling flares. Today's popular propellant is called "smokeless powder," but it is not smokeless and not even a true powder. Gelatinized cellulose nitrate is an example. Another form, ballistite (bal-iss-tight), is used as a rocket propellant. It is made up of two explosive substances, nitroglycerin and nitrocellulose (night-ro-sell-u-lowse)—also known as collodion—as well as camphor.

Besides their military uses, explosives are employed in mining, quarrying, and the demolition of buildings, bridges, and other structures. They are also used for fireworks, airbags in automobiles, mountain carvings (like Mount Rushmore), and even in medicine to break up kidney and gallstones.

The United Nations classifies the hazards of explosive materials and explosive components into six divisions:

1. Mass explosion
2. Non-mass explosion that produces fragments
3. Mass fire with a minor blast or fragment
4. Moderate fire with no blast or fragment
5. Very insensitive explosive substance with a mass explosion hazard
6. Extremely insensitive explosive article

CASE STUDY **CHERNOBYL**

The world's worst accidental explosion happened at the Chernobyl power plant on April 26, 1986, in the Ukraine, then part of the Union of Soviet Socialist Republics (USSR). A nuclear chain reaction went out of control, causing several explosions that blew away the reactor's heavy steel and concrete lid. This followed a sudden increase in temperature that caused part of the fuel to rupture into a steam explosion that destroyed the reactor core.

The Chernobyl disaster killed fifty-six people directly, and the escaping radiation resulted in the evacuation of about 135,000 people. The radiation spread around the world, even reaching parts of the United States. The World Health Organization estimates that the disaster has since caused a further 9,000 related deaths from cancer and other diseases. Greenpeace believes the total deaths are more than 200,000.

Chernobyl's deadly doses of radiation turned an active community into a ghost town. The unit that exploded is now encased in a thick concrete chamber.

chapter 2

What Can Fires Tell Investigators?

The work of skilled fire investigators can pinpoint the source of a fire and uncover evidence that indicates signs of a crime.

A trained fire investigator can uncover many clues about the origin of a fire and whether a crime has been committed. Locating the fire's point of origin, or "seat," can reveal how it started and spread. But finding evidence of arson, also called an incendiary fire, is more of a challenge. It is vital to the community to catch an arsonist. Sniffer dogs and instruments can detect **accelerants** used to start and intensify a fire, such as gasoline or kerosene. Arson might be suspected if the owner removed personal property or a commercial inventory before the fire began.

If investigators find a body, they will search for signs of smoke inhalation, such as particles in the victim's lungs; if they find none, they will conclude that death occurred before the fire broke out. Detectives will then search for underlying bleeding or other injuries on the body. When fire investigators testify as witnesses in trials, they are generally allowed to present the

◁ **Firefighters put their lives in danger to save lives and property. They must face flames, smoke, explosions, and buildings that might collapse.**

KEY FACTS **ASSOCIATIONS**

Fire and arson investigation associations provide professional training, public education and advice, and communication between their members. The U.S. Fire Administration (USFA) researches and publishes information on fire

Proper training gives firefighters the knowledge and confidence that one day might save their lives and help them rescue others.

prevention and offers training at its National Fire Academy in Emmitsburgh, Maryland. This includes how to investigate fires, prevent and control arson, and develop interview and testimony skills. The Bureau of Alcohol, Tobacco, Firearms and Explosives (ATF) enforces Federal laws and regulations regarding arson and explosives and offers training at its Glenco, Georgia, facility. The National Association of Fire Investigators has both regional and national training programs. The National Association of State Fire Marshals exchanges information among its members. Ohio is home to the oldest fire marshal's office (established in 1906), with eight bureaus, including a forensic laboratory and investigation bureau. The International Association of Arson Investigators (IAAI), with about 9,000 members worldwide, publishes information on new detection methods and has a Fire and Arson Career Development School.

physical evidence they found but cannot say if the fire was definitely arson. In Virginia courts, for instance, the fire expert can give opinions on where the fire started, the cause or source of ignition, how it proceeded, and if it is possible to eliminate certain accidental causes. The court, however, must permit the jurors to draw their own conclusions as to the cause of the fire. For that reason, a fire investigator tends to use words carefully—for example, saying burn patterns found at the scene "are consistent with the presence of an accelerant."

Death by Fire

Fires are damaging and deadly. According to the National Fire Protection Association, in 2004, 395,500 home fires were reported in the United States, which resulted in 3,190 deaths, 13,700 injured, and $5.8 billion in direct property damage. Although 96 percent of U.S. households have at least one smoke detector, about 70 percent of the deaths occur in homes with no alarms or working alarms.

Fire investigators also put their lives on the line. In 2000, in New York City, a collapsing chimney crushed one man while he was examining a fire scene. In the same year, another investigator had a heart attack at a fire scene in Ticonderoga, New York. Les McPhree, an investigator in the Ontario Fire Marshal's Office, died of cancer in 2006 after a career of sifting through the smoldering rubble of 3,000 fires in eastern Ontario, looking for clues. Although he wore a dust mask during his final years on the job, McPhree was certain that the hazards of his job caused his cancer.

When the death toll from a fire is high, the authorities launch in-depth investigations. Often, the facts are obvious, such as in the 2003 fire in The Station nightclub in West Warwick, Rhode Island, which killed 100 concertgoers. Onstage pyrotechnics used by the band Great White sparked a blaze that ignited highly flammable soundproofing foam, and the fire spread rapidly.

In other cases, the facts may not be firmly established but investigators may form a theory based on experience. The 1985 fire at a soccer stadium in Bradford, England, killed fifty-six people. It began as a small fire in the stands but, in just four minutes, the flames spread to the roof. The forensic scientist, Dr. David Woolley, said the possible source was a match or cigarette dropped into a polystyrene cup.

KEY FACTS **BECOMING AN INVESTIGATOR**

To investigate fires a person must want to explore, detect, and determine the truth. Fire investigators seek the origin and cause of a fire, as well as whether the fire was accidental or deliberately set. In many communities, they have the power to arrest suspected arsonists. The road to becoming a fire investigator usually begins locally, perhaps as an employee or volunteer in a fire or police department. This can lead to the national level, where the Bureau of Alcohol, Tobacco, Firearms and Explosives (ATF) employs approximately eighty certified fire investigators, who undergo a two-year training program. The Federal Bureau of Investigation (FBI) also provides fire training for agents.

A career in the private sector is another option—for example, working for insurance companies investigating claims for fire damage. Potential candidates, whether for public or private employment, often have taken college courses in engineering, forensics, science, and photography. Some schools, such as the University of Maryland and Oklahoma State University, offer a curriculum in fire science.

The charred remains of a fire become critical evidence in the hands of a professional fire investigator looking for clues of arson.

After firefighters leave the scene, investigators move in to sift through the debris. Their attention to detail can turn the area into a crime scene.

How Fires Spread

A house fire set deliberately expands and moves differently than an accidental one. It progresses much more rapidly because arsonists normally set fires in multiple locations and use accelerants to spread the flames—almost certainly guaranteeing that it will be a bigger fire.

In three out of ten cases, the fire begins in the kitchen and follows the path of least resistance, so it prefers open doors and windows to closed ones. Fire always travels upward, so arson would seem likely if the fire followed a track across a floor. By noting the fire's path, an investigator can work backward or downward to the source. The clues will include char patterns, heat shadows, and the direction of the melt. Accidental fires normally show a distinct source, whereas the source or sources of an arson fire may be obscured.

Arson is more difficult to detect in a forest fires, whose path is determined by trees, undergrowth, weather, and wind. The answer again involves locating the origin, where an arsonist's accelerant or other materials may be discovered.

Investigating the Causes of Fire

Determining the cause of a fire often looks impossible, because most or all of the evidence may have been destroyed. Water used to fight the fire causes further damage. Evidence might also be contaminated, moved, or destroyed by the many people on the scene, such as the police, rescue and emergency workers, health and safety officers, the press, and the public. The homeowner might also destroy evidence by trying to salvage possessions after the fire.

One way to protect evidence is by flagging it with markers or cones. Items or areas can be covered with clean boxes or tarpaulins and isolated by barrier tape, rope, or barricades. An investigator might also draw sketches of the area and record observations in a notebook or on tape.

In an investigation, there may be some confusion about who, exactly, is supposed to do what. The fire department will try to establish the fire's cause, as will the owner's insurance company. If arson is suspected, a law enforcement authority has to investigate and subsequently bring in the state fire marshal or even a federal agency.

A trained fire investigator, however, arrives early and begins by questioning bystanders who might know where and when the fire started. After the fire is extinguished and the building judged safe from collapse and poisonous fumes, the investigator can sift through the debris, looking for the smallest evidence that could reveal whether the blaze was accidental or set on purpose. The renowned forensic scientist Dr. Henry C. Lee, who is an expert on identifying accelerants, says: "With an arson scene, we can capture the vapor and do the analysis before the investigator leaves the scene. I can tell if it's gasoline, kerosene, or any other accelerant."

One of the latest aids in investigations of crimes such as arson is teleforensics, which uses advanced technology to allow experts to view the crime scene, even though they might be hundreds of miles away. Images of the scene are digitized and transmitted electronically to connect several investigators with the scene and with one another. The experts swap suggestions that lead to the best analysis.

The Bureau of Alcohol, Tobacco, Firearms and Explosives (ATF) has a Fire Research Laboratory that is the first facility in the world dedicated to fire scene investigations, including the ability to reconstruct fire scenes to find out how they began and spread. It conducts analysis of fire ignition, accelerants, and the fire pattern. A computerized model of the fire is used to calculate the physics and function of fire.

A good starting point is to find the fire's place of origin—its "seat." The flames normally go up and out, making a V burn pattern, with the bottom indicating where they started. If there are more than one of these burn marks, someone could have lit several fires around the room or building. Accidental fires almost always start in one place.

Sometimes the ignition source is obvious, such as a stove, wastebasket, or candle. Clues can include intense charring and ceiling damage, and any patterns of smoke or the building's collapse. An investigator should search for items used by an arsonist, such as matchbooks, cigarettes, candles, Molotov cocktails, chemical masses fused together, or any mechanical or electronic device, such as an electronic timer.

It is more difficult to decide whether these were part of a criminal act. Did a candle, for instance, fall onto a newspaper accidentally or did an arsonist place it there? Why was it lit? Was it placed in a dangerous location? Investigators need to be skillful in interviewing those connected with the fire and judging their reactions. Ordinary witnesses are also valuable. They might testify that a fire consisted almost entirely of flames, which suggests arson, since accidental fires usually produce a good amount of smoke before flaming.

One tip-off to a crime is the discovery of an accelerant, such as gasoline or paint thinners, used to boost the fire. (Sometimes an arsonist is amazingly careless.

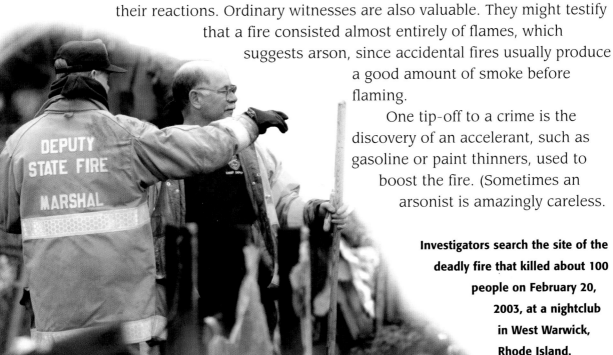

Investigators search the site of the deadly fire that killed about 100 people on February 20, 2003, at a nightclub in West Warwick, Rhode Island.

DEPUTY
STATE FIRE
MARSHAL

It would seem foolish to leave an incriminating gas can with fingerprints at the back of a house, but it has happened.) Any accelerant left unburned will leave a characteristic odor, and liquid accelerants will leave their own pool marks on the floor. An arson examiner collects debris from a scene, and packages it securely, since accelerants evaporate.

Investigators also carry instruments to the scene: a gas analysis kit contains crystals that change color if traces of an accelerant are detected in the air; a **hydrocarbon** vapor detector draws in air to a hydrogen flame that rises if an accelerant is present; and a portable photo ionization monitor, which is a tube that uses **ultraviolet light** to identify accelerants like benzene and xylene (*zy-leen*). Samples are sent to labs where technicians can identify gasoline, oils, and **solvents**, though usually not the specific brands. The technicians normally link together **gas chromatography** and **mass spectrometry** instruments to identify the accelerant by breaking its chemicals into ions (electrically charged atoms) and accelerating them in a magnetic field to produce a spectrum with unique bands.

K-9 Units

In the United States, more than 200 arson dog teams, or specialized K-9 units, sniff out accelerants at fire scenes. The ATF Canine Detection Program also uses them to find explosives and spent cartridge cases. Dog handlers train the dogs by rewarding them with food when they identify hidden samples and notify their handlers. Investigators **calibrate** a dog's nose (200 times more sensitive than a human's) by putting a scent on an item and ordering it to find that odor. Dogs can detect tiny amounts of accelerants that even machines miss, as well as many types of combustibles, such as gasoline, diesel, and lighter fluid, long after a fire has been extinguished. They can cover a fire scene and areas just outside it twice as fast as a human. In 2001, in an arson case in Iowa, a dog identified on the porch of a burned building an accelerant that even laboratory testing could not detect. Testimony was accepted in court that a dog's nose is much more sensitive than lab equipment.

Dogs are also used in crowd searches, because most arsonists take pride in viewing their fire. The fire inspector walks the dog among the onlookers so that it can sniff out any accelerants still on the arsonist's clothes. Even when suspects are identified later, a dog can detect odors lingering on the person's clothes.

After the fire has started, its behavior is important to investigators, who will attempt to retrace its spread. Did it progress to open windows and doors, which is normal, or did someone force it into a less likely direction? Did the fire go upward or did it burn across the floor, indicating an accelerant? A fire investigator checks for burn trails made by cloth or paper, and trails on carpeted or hardwood floors. A fire is also suspicious if it began and moved very quickly.

A fire investigator can also detect a crime by using simple observation. A forced entry and exit might be evident, or the sprinkler or alarm systems might have been turned off or deliberately disabled.

K-9 units have become a familiar sight at major fires and explosions. Their sense of smell is 200 times more powerful than that of humans.

Blood Sampling

One of the most difficult fires to investigate is arson set from the outside. The signs are evident from scorch marks, but the arsonist quickly disappears without leaving traces within the building. Still unsolved is the 2002 home fire in Rankin County, Mississippi, that killed the Reverend Sammy McDonald, his wife, and three boys. "It was an outside cause," said the firefighter Greg Ecklund. "It wasn't an electrical fire; it wasn't a fire caused by natural occurrences. It

TOOLS **ARSON DETECTIVE'S EQUIPMENT**

Arson investigators should have a tool kit with the necessary equipment to probe the scene and identify, collect, and preserve evidence for laboratory analysis, further investigations, and court proceedings. The standard detective equipment ranges from simple tape to sophisticated electronic devices. Larger departments might add a sniffer dog or portable photo ionization monitor. Some basic but necessary tools include:

- Barrier tape to keep others away from the scene being investigated
- Clean unused evidence containers, such as cans, glass jars, or polyester bags
- Evidence tags, labels, and tape
- Marker flags or cones
- Gloves, both disposable and work types
- Hand tools such as hammers, screwdrivers, knives, and crowbars
- Rakes, brooms, spades, etc.
- Flashlights and spotlights
- Digital still and video cameras and accessories
- Writing equipment, such as notebooks, pens, pencils, and permanent markers
- Personal protective clothing and equipment

It may not be the easiest job, but arson investigators know the correct tools can reveal evidence that will lead to a conviction.

Matches that are carelessly discarded by an arsonist may survive the fire and become key evidence for the prosecution.

wasn't a gas leak or anything like that." In such cases, investigators look for shoeprints or tire marks, but they are often entirely dependent on witnesses.

When a fire includes a death, an autopsy can determine whether the victim died before the fire. In the 2006 trial of serial killer Paul Runge in Chicago, the court heard testimony that no soot was found in the lungs of a mother and daughter he had murdered in their bed before setting it on fire. Runge was convicted and sentenced to death.

Samples of blood can also be tested to reveal whether carbon monoxide is present, meaning the person was breathing after the fire began. The person conducting the autopsy also looks for **vital reactions**. If a victim was alive in a fire, the body will have responded by activating leucocytes *(look-o-sites)*— white blood cells—causing inflammation. It is also possible to test blisters by heating them in the lab. If the person was alive, the protein within the blister will solidify. If the body shows laceration wounds, it is difficult to decide whether the heat or a physical attack caused them. However, a lab exam will reveal whether blood vessels and nerves below the surface are injured, meaning the person has been attacked.

When bodies are found at a fire scene, they should be left undisturbed until the proper police procedures are followed. The same applies to trace evidence, such as hair, fibers, fingerprints, and blood. The fire investigator can also help detect evidence of crimes other than arson, indicated by the presence of drugs or weapons. Specialized investigations are needed for vehicle fires. Automobiles and trucks are mechanically complex, so a fire investigator should work with a mechanic to find the cause of the fire. If the vehicle was removed to a police compound before it was examined, an investigator needs to visit the site of the burning, hunt for an accelerant, and even search the surrounding area for accelerant containers. Any gas, oil, and other liquids should be collected and sent to a lab for testing. Equally complex problems are involved in the burning of boats and ships.

chapter 3

Arson Cases

Cases of intentionally set fires are difficult to solve. However, many arsonists are caught through the hard work of investigators.

Every year in the United States, fires set by arsonists kill more than 4,000 people and injure 20,000 others. Among the victims are 300 children who die, one-third by fires they set themselves, and 3,000 others who are injured. In 2005, the average loss of value for each offense was $15,000, but the average loss for industrial and manufacturing buildings was $360,000. Arson accounts for half of recorded fires in Britain (90 percent in some areas) and costs that nation's economy £2.8 billion (U.S. $5.2 billion) a year.

Arson is a difficult crime to solve. The Federal Bureau of Investigation (FBI) reports that clearance (crimes solved) for 2005 was only 18.3 percent of the 67,504 offenses reported. Some cities improved their higher clearance records after developing strong anti-arson programs. Charlotte, North Carolina, consistently maintains a 30 percent rate since it set up a fire investigation task force. This force has several

◁ The ruins of a fire will appear to have destroyed any evidence, but the fire's path and the presence of accelerants are clues of arson.

33

agencies working side by side at fire scenes, bringing together fire investigators from the city's fire department, arson detectives from the police department, agents from the state's Bureau of Investigation, and agents from the U.S. Bureau of Alcohol, Tobacco, Firearms and Explosives (ATF).

The National Fire Incident Reporting System (NFIRS) defines arson as an act to "unlawfully and intentionally damage, or attempt to damage, any real or personal property by fire or incendiary device." Other definitions include purposely setting a fire that accidentally gets out of control.

Members of the San Diego Fire Department's Metro Arson Strike Team look for clues after a fire destroyed this 206-unit condominium.

CASE STUDY **A SERIAL ARSONIST**

He is the man called "the most prolific and devastating arsonist in California State history" and "probably the most prolific American arsonist of the twentieth century." He committed a series of attacks in January 1987 in California's San Joaquin Valley and another series in March 1989 along the California coast.

Astonishingly, he was Captain John Orr, the fire investigator for the city of Glendale. His first fire, in a shopping plaza, killed four people, including a two-year-old child. When arson investigators said the source was an electrical fire, Orr stepped in to declare it was arson. Captain Marvin G. Casey of the Bakersfield Fire Department rightly suspected the arsonist was an arson investigator. Both series of fires had occurred near conferences held by arson investigators.

Finally, Orr's fingerprint was found at one scene. More evidence came from his unpublished novel, *Point of Origin*, which describes the same type of arson attack. His mistake was giving it to the Glendale fire marshal for approval, since his department was mentioned. Orr is now serving ten years in a federal prison before being transferred to a state prison for a life sentence.

John Orr used his knowledge as a fire investigator to start fires and outwit other arson investigators, but even he made crucial mistakes.

Profiling Arsonists

Arson is traditionally classified into six types according to its frequency. The first three types are for a single fire at, respectively, one, two, or three locations. In the fourth type, three or more fires at the same place and time are classified as "mass arson." In the fifth, three or more at different locations without a cooling-off period is called "spree arson," while in the sixth, three or more at different places with some time between them is classified as "serial arson." The fascination that some young people have with fire can lead to arson. Children as young as two can start to play with fire—for example, burning toys or paper. At this age, fire-play and setting fires are more innocent acts, but they can lead to the more malicious use of fire to destroy something or hurt someone.

Teenagers age twelve to seventeen are responsible for more than 50 percent of arson cases in Canada, according to the Hospital for Sick Children, which is part of the University of Toronto. The hospital states that at least 50 percent of boys will play or experiment with fire at least once during their childhood or adolescence; however, only one girl does so for every nine boys. Police records reveal that arson committed by juveniles, who tend to brag, is easier to solve than cases involving adults, who keep it to themselves. An FBI report states that 90 percent of arsonists are white males.

Anti-Arsonist Programs

Many U.S. cities have programs designed to stop juveniles from setting fires. One of the best is the Phoenix (Arizona) Fire Department's Youth Firesetter Prevention Program. If someone age eight to eighteen sets a fire intentionally, he or she will be given fire safety education and counseling if it is a first offense. If it is a felony arson or repeat offense, the youth is prosecuted. If the fire was accidental due to curiosity, experimentation, or negligence, the offender is recommended to attend the youth fire safety class on a voluntary basis.

The wide range in age, background, and personality makes it difficult to draw a profile of an average arsonist. One perpetrator might be someone calm and methodical defrauding his insurance company. Another might be a frenzied, compulsive pyromaniac. Those convicted have ranged from honor students to those who have previously committed other offenses. David Berkowitz set at least 1,488 fires around New York City before becoming the infamous "Son of Sam" serial killer in the late 1970s, murdering seven women and wounding others before being caught and sentenced to 365 years in prison.

Another problem with profiling is that few arsonists are caught. In the FBI study, "The Firesetter: A Psychological Profile," bureau agent Anthony Olen Rider

CASE STUDY **A SUBDIVISION FIRE**

The largest residential arson case in Maryland's history happened on December 6, 2004, when thirty-five houses in the Hunter's Brooke subdivision at Indian Head, an expensive suburb of Washington, D.C., were torched. Damage amounted to more than $10 million, but nobody was hurt because the houses were under construction.

Fire investigators knew immediately that this was arson because the fire's intensity suggested ignitable liquids were used. These were found at several houses, which indicated the involvement of more than one person. Interviewers found that the security guard had left the site early before the flames began. The guard, Aaron Speed, and four others who had participated in the crime were arrested. They confessed to pouring flammable materials into buckets, bottles, and plastic containers, and setting them off with flares, matches, lighters, and propane torches. In this case, there were several motives. Speed said he was angry with his company for not giving him bereavement leave after his child died, and he also was jealous of the wealthy residents. Another of the arsonists, Jeremy Parady, said he participated because African Americans were buying many of the homes.

The Hunter's Brooke subdivision was lined with expensive houses that were a temptation to arsonists who had worked there and even guarded the property.

says that "a typical firesetter just does not exist" because the low numbers caught and convicted make it impossible to establish a profile. (About two individuals are convicted for every 100 reported incendiary or suspicious fires.) Psychologist Joel Dvoskin, a member of the American Board of Forensic Psychology, noted in an interview: "It could be that the smarter people get away with it, and less smart people are more likely to get caught."

Psychologists who work with young arsonists have found that many do have below-average intelligence, but Dr. Alan Feldberg of the Cornell Abraxas Group in Pennsylvania said about one-fifth of young offenders have college-level reading ability. "Some are extremely computer-savvy," he added, "and learn in a scientific way how to set fires to get maximum impact."

Two students from Birmingham-Southern College, Russell DeBusk (left) and Ben Moseley, were arrested for the burning of several Alabama churches in 2006.

The motives of arsonists are easier to define, though they have changed over the last three decades. Arson used to be primarily for profit, with insurance companies as the main victims. Crimes against people have now overtaken crime against property. Investigators from the U.S. Fire Administration have found that spite and revenge now dominate as motives for arson, especially when there are casualties. Most arsonists, therefore, use fire as a weapon to harm specific people, and this includes domestic violence cases. The second most frequent motive is vandalism, followed by fraud, and then crime concealment.

A specialized category is terrorism arson, such as eco-terrorism arson. These firesetters usually work in groups, use special devices, and seek publicity for their causes. One group active in the United States is the Earth Liberation Front, which has set several fires, including a $12 million blaze in 1998 that destroyed a ski resort in Vail, Colorado, and a fire in 2001 that destroyed the Center for Urban Horticulture at the University of Washington in Seattle. In Britain, the Animal Liberation Front (ALF) has been behind arson attacks. In 2005, after the ALF used an incendiary device to burn the car of an executive from a Canadian company involved with Huntingdon, a second Canadian firm dropped a client doing business with Huntingdon Life Sciences, an animal-testing firm that operates in Britain and the United States.

Random Arson

The most difficult arson cases to solve are random acts. A deliberately set fire is easier to trace if the offender was trying to collect insurance, destroy records, ruin a competitor, exact revenge, target groups (blacks, abortionists, etc.), or cover up another crime. An arson attack without a clear motive leaves fire investigators with few clues.

This was the case in a series of nighttime church fires in Alabama in 2006. Five Baptist churches were burned on February 3 and four more on February 7. A racial motive was not evident, because four of the church congregations were white and five were black. Fire investigators did not have to sift through debris to know this was arson, but no clues were left in the churches—five destroyed, four damaged—that would point to suspects. The only evidence was a set of tire tracks, which Bibb County Sheriff Keith Hannah immediately protected. He was also on the phone shortly after his discovery to bring in the state fire marshal and the ATF. Investigators found the same tracks outside five of the other fires.

The federal, state, and local investigators then combed through approximately 1,000 leads, interviewed 1,500 people, and inspected 500 cars, before linking the tire types to a particular store in Pelham, Alabama. One of their customers was the mother of one of the three youths later arrested; she had purchased four tires for her sports utility vehicle. After becoming a suspect, her son admitted to his father that he was at the fires.

The three youths were college students from the Birmingham area: Matthew Lee Cloyd, age twenty (whose mother had bought the tires); Benjamin Nathan Moseley, nineteen (who confessed); and Russell Lee DeBusk, Jr., also nineteen. They told federal agents that they set the first blazes as a joke, and the others to throw investigators off the track. It is virtually impossible to solve a fire started as "a joke," by outsiders from a distant city, but investigators in this case could fall back on basic forensic science to trace back the tire tracks.

Colorado's Worst Wildfire

Some fires burn for an incredibly long time. The Hayman fire began in Colorado's Pike National Forest on June 8, 2002, and was not extinguished until twenty-one days later. It burned 137,000 acres (55,485 hectares) over four counties, destroying 133 homes, one building, and 484 outbuildings, with the cost of the damage reaching nearly $40 million. At the peak of the fire, 2,564 firefighters battled the flames.

An unlikely arsonist had started the worst wildfire in the state's history. Terry Barton, a forest service employee, was patrolling the forest to enforce a fire ban, when she decided to burn a letter from her estranged husband. She did this within a designated campfire ring, but a severe drought had made it a no-fire zone, which she knew. The blaze spread rapidly despite her efforts to contain it.

Barton first said she had smelled a campfire and found it out of control. Fire inspectors, however, reported that she could not have smelled smoke from the distance she described, and the fire would have been a different size when she allegedly discovered it. After confessing, Barton received a sentence of twelve years in prison on state charges to be served concurrently with a six-year federal sentence.

Arson can create monstrous fires in a forest, where the flames have virtually unlimited fuel and can change direction in minutes.

Investigating and Collecting Evidence

Motive is often also missing in cases of wildfires set on purpose. Sometimes, they are started when someone tries to set a house on fire out of revenge. Then there is the strange "vanity fire," when someone starts a fire in order to point it out and become a hero. Even some firefighters have been convicted of this crime. A former forest service worker, Tamara Meredith, was sentenced to more than three years in prison in 1999 for setting a string of forest fires in Oregon's Umpqua National Forest in order to earn overtime fighting them.

KEY FACTS | **FIGHTING WILDFIRES**

Wildfires are vicious, fanned by winds that supply extra oxygen, and are surrounded by an abundance of fuel in the form of trees, underbrush, leaves, and grassy fields. In an average year, they consume about 5 million acres (2 million hectares) in the United States. Their unpredictable quality can make them deadly. During an arson fire in southern California in October 2006, a shift in the winds suddenly pushed a wall of flames around five firefighters trying to save a house. Four died and the other was hospitalized with serious burns over most of his body.

Firefighting tackles one or more parts of the fire triangle: heat, fuel, and oxygen. Air tankers help to cool down a fire by dropping thousands of gallons of water or chemical retardants onto the flames. Helicopters can also be used to do this, but on a smaller scale. Firefighters deny fuel to a wildfire by putting in firebreaks—usually by digging trenches or creating clearings—or by starting backfires (fires designed to burn up untouched flammable material), which burn up potential fuels before the raging wildfire arrives. Firefighters can deny a fire oxygen by coating would-be fuel with fire-retardant chemicals.

A good way to contain a wildfire is to attack it immediately. Smokejumpers are specialized firefighters who parachute out of planes into a remote area to fight a small wildfire before it grows.

National Guardsmen from many surrounding regions are often called in to work alongside professional firefighters in battling a dangerous wildfire.

Debris left by arsonists can be sent for laboratory examinations, and those arrested can face state or federal charges, including murder. It takes about a year to put together a strong case against a suspected arsonist. Those who start random wildfires, however, are seldom caught. A wildfire called the Old Fire was sparked in the San Bernardino Mountains of California on October 25, 2003, when (according to witnesses) occupants of a white van threw flaming objects out of the passenger's window; the suspects were never apprehended. The fire killed six people, burned 91,281 acres (36,969 hectares), and destroyed 993 homes.

Sentencing is difficult when an intentional small fire accidentally expands into a wildfire. Two days after the Old Fire began, a hunter named Sergio Martinez became lost in California's Cleveland National Forest. He set brush and timber alight as a signal, but it billowed into the Cedar Fire, one of the state's worst wildfires in history, killing fourteen people, including a firefighter, destroying 2,820 homes and other buildings, and burning 280,278 acres (113,513 hectares). At one point, the blaze was consuming 2 acres (0.8 hectare) per second. For this, Martinez received a sentence of six months in a correctional center, 960 hours of community service, and five years' probation, and was ordered to pay $150 a month over five years to educate hunters and hikers.

Fire in Court

Juries in arson cases can hear conflicting testimony from fire investigators for the prosecution and defense. This was the case when George Souliotes, a landlord in Modesto, California, was tried in 1997 on charges relating to a fire that killed his tenant and her two children. He had tried to evict them, and the state also argued he wanted to collect insurance money. Arson investigators for the prosecution testified that a medium petroleum distillate, a substance that is sometimes flammable, was found on both Souliotes' shoes and carpeting in the house. The defense had its own arson expert, who testified that the fire could have been caused by a faulty stove. After this conflicting testimony, the trial ended in a hung jury.

In 1999, Souliotes was convicted in a second trial, but since then arson investigators have analyzed the data from the scene once again and now conclusively say that the medium petroleum distillate found on his shoes was not the same substance found at the scene. Souliotes is now in prison serving a life sentence, but a legal firm and the Northern California Innocence Project are attempting to secure his release.

Fire inspectors have a lot of experience in punching holes in suspects' testimony. Herbert Landry, a Hurricane Katrina evacuee in Provo, Utah, tried to explain away a fire that occurred in his apartment (funded by the Federal Emergency Management Agency) on February 26, 2006. He had been served with an eviction order and was to have moved his belongings out by the day of the fire. The fire damaged eight other units and caused $183,000 in damage. Landry said he had thrown a party the day before during which some alcohol was spilled. Then, a friend came over the next day and smoked cigarettes while seated at the edge of his bed, setting the alcohol on fire. Provo Fire Marshal Jim Guynn, however, testified that a cigarette lit a day after alcohol had been spilled would never cause a fire. Burn patterns were also discovered that were consistent with the use of an accelerant, and Landy was convicted of arson.

In some rare cases, fire investigators fail to collect the proper evidence. In a high-profile case in September 2006 in Allegheny County, Pennsylvania, a former school board member, Beverly Jo Coon, was tried for drugging her boyfriend, a former school superintendent, and setting his apartment on fire in 2005. The defense attacked the Allegheny County investigators, saying that they had sent nothing from the scene for laboratory analysis and saved no evidence from the fire. One of the jurors later said they had been troubled by the quality of the county fire marshal's investigation. In spite of this, Coon was convicted of arson and

Children must be taught early to avoid playing with matches. The habit can develop into a fascination with fire and even lead to arson.

KEY FACTS — THE DEADLIEST FIRES

The 10 deadliest fires in the United States between 1957 and 2006 were:

DEATHS	PLACE	DATE
164	Nightclub in Southgate, Kentucky	May 28, 1977
100	Nightclub in Warwick, Rhode Island	February 20, 2003
95	School in Chicago, Illinois	December 1, 1958
87	Social club in the Bronx, New York	March 25, 1990
84	MGM Grand Hotel in Las Vegas, Nevada	November 21, 1980
72	Nursing home in Warrenton, Missouri	February 17, 1957
72	Religious cult compound at Waco, Texas	April 19, 1993
63	Rest home in Fitchville, Ohio	November 23, 1963
42	Jail in Columbia, Tennessee	June 26, 1977
37	State prison in Jay, Florida	July 16, 1967

attempted **homicide** based on circumstantial evidence—she had behaved obsessively toward her married victim, and a narcotic was found in his blood after she had fed him pastries.

Investigators sometimes give a preliminary verdict on an accidental fire but keep searching for clues. In 2005, in Cleveland, Ohio, a horrific fire killed an adult and eight children, the largest single-event mass murder in that city's history. After labeling it an accident, fire investigators continued to comb for evidence for two weeks. Their persistence paid off when they uncovered gasoline used in the crime. Although ten arson and homicide investigators remain on the case, no arrests have yet been made.

chapter 4

A History of Explosives

Explosives have been used since ancient times, but discoveries have greatly increased their power through the years.

Long before the use of explosives, fire was employed in warfare in the form of flaming arrows and fire posts. The Greeks of Byzantium used **Greek fire**, also called "wild fire," a sort of liquid petroleum that could burn in water. It was used to successfully defend Constantinople in 673 C.E. by spraying it from bronze tubes fixed on the prows of the Greek ships and setting the enemy's ships on fire. The idea of projecting fire at the enemy continued through Word War II with the use of flamethrowers.

This changed when the Chinese military began to experiment with gunpowder, or black powder, which was supposedly discovered around the tenth century by an **alchemist** looking for a mythical potion of eternal life for the emperor. The mixture was of charcoal, saltpeter (potassium nitrate), and sulfur. The Chinese military first used it at the end of fire lances and arrows. About the same time, Arabs were filling glass and

◁ **Despite strict safety rules for mines in the United States, controlled underground explosions can be a danger if they detonate prematurely.**

earthenware grenade-type weapons with gasoline. By 1050, China had created fireworks. Around 1100, crude guns that looked like small bulbous cannons began to appear. They used gunpowder with a high nitrate content to fire a projectile from a metal barrel. Also around this time, Arab merchants introduced grenades to the Chinese, who then developed their own versions. Within a decade, the Chinese were filling bombs with gunpowder and firing them from iron catapults. By 1132, they were starting to use round musket-type bullets.

Around 1150, the first rockets appeared in China and within thirty years military rockets were being produced. In 1232, the Mongols besieged the northern Chinese city of Kaifeng *(kay-fang)*, bombarding it with metal bombs filled with gunpowder. By the mid thirteenth century, the Chinese had started putting black powder in bamboo tubes to propel stones.

Although the Chinese vigorously guarded the recipe, gunpowder, called "Chinese snow," had spread to the West and south India by the thirteenth century, along with fireworks. In 1242, the English friar and scientist Roger Bacon published the formula for gunpowder. By the middle of the century, Islamic armies were using gunpowder against the Crusaders in Palestine, and their weapons included grenades. Arabs also invented an advanced trebuchet *(tray-boo-shay)*—a medieval weapon for throwing large stones—that employed counterweights to hurl missiles and exploding bombs. By 1276, the trebuchet was being used to lay siege to Chinese cities.

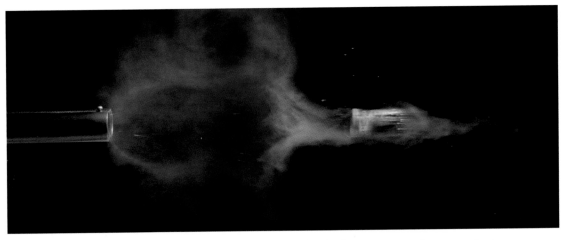

A bullet is propelled from a gun by a low-initiating explosive known as a primary explosive. Black gunpowder served this purpose for centuries.

KEY FACTS — U.S. EXPLOSIVES TIMELINE

1675	The nation's first black powder mill opens in Milton, Massachusetts.
1750	Benjamin Franklin compresses and encases black powder into cartridges.
1818–21	Black powder is first used to excavate a road tunnel in Pennsylvania.
1830	Moses Shaw of New York patents an electric firing device for black powder.
1860	About 25 million lbs (11 million kg) of black powder are produced just before the Civil War.
1870	The nation's first dynamite plant, the Giant Powder Company, opens in San Francisco.
1907	More than 287 million lbs (129 million kg) of black powder are used in the United States.
1948	The first explosion is used to begin carving the Crazy Horse Memorial into Thunder Mountain in South Dakota.
1957	About 100 million lbs (45 million kg) of explosives are used for underground explosions.
1959	The United States has thirty-nine dynamite plants operating.
1991	Texan Paul "Red" Adair and his men use explosives to extinguish 117 oil well fires ignited by Iraqi troops retreating from Kuwait.
1995	Only one dynamite plant remains in the United States.

Gunpowder for War and Mining

By the turn of the fourteenth century, the Chinese had created mobile artillery units for the battlefield, and by 1332 they were propelling rockets by gunpowder. At the same time, Western countries were introducing basic cannons fired by gunpowder. About 1320, the German Franciscan monk Berthold Schwarz was making practical guns. "Schwarz" (black) was added to his name because of his experiments with gunpowder. Among the earliest images of a cannon were drawings in Florence, Italy, in 1326, and in Scotland a year later. In 1453, the Ottoman Turks used gigantic cannons with barrels nearly 3 feet (1 meter) wide in their successful siege of Constantinopole. These weapons could hurl a 700-lb (315-kg) cannonball more than a mile. The Ottoman Empire also produced the first musket with a steel barrel in 1595. Europeans were using gunpowder for firework celebrations by 1540, and for mining by 1600. By 1670, German miners had introduced powder to tin mines in Cornwall, England. The first large use of gunpowder in civil engineering was in 1679 to excavate the Malpas Tunnel in France for a canal. Its first use for a road tunnel was from 1818 to 1821 in Pennsylvania in the United States.

In 1700, Russia became a leader in producing cast-iron cannons. By about 1750, India was also making inventive weapons by fashioning unused cannon materials into long matchlock muskets that could be fired from a sitting position. By 1785, Indian military rockets weighed up to 9 lbs (4 kg) and could be fired more than 3,200 ft (about 1,000 m). In 1750, in the United States, the inventor Benjamin Franklin devised a way to compress gunpowder and put it in cartridges. Eighty years later, New York inventor Moses Shaw patented an electrical ignition system for gunpowder.

Deadly Discoveries

In 1831, an English leather merchant, William Bickford, invented the "miner's safety fuse," which made black powder much safer. Miners had suffered frequent accidents when planned explosions detonated prematurely. Bickford tried several combinations before discovering that flax yarn with a gunpowder core made a reliable slow-burning fuse.

In 1846, the German-Swiss chemist Christian Frederick Schonbein (1799–1868) accidentally discovered guncotton, later called nitrocellulose (see Chapter 1, page 18). Although his wife had forbidden him from experimenting at home, he did so in the kitchen when she was away. One day he spilled a mixture of nitric acid and sulfuric acid, and mopped it up with his wife's cotton apron. Hanging it over the oven to dry, he was shocked when it ignited with an explosion and virtually vanished. The two acids had reacted with the cellulose fibers in the cotton to produce guncotton. Schonbein recognized the importance

PROFILE **ALFRED NOBEL**

The inventor of dynamite was born in 1833 in Stockholm, Sweden, the son of an engineer. While still a child, he moved to Russia, where his father, an explosives expert, was testing an underwater mine he had invented. Alfred went to Paris to study chemistry and then lived for a while in the United States to work with another Swedish native, John Ericsson, who invented the Civil War ironclad ship, the *Monitor*. Nobel returned to Sweden in 1859 and began developing a safe and manageable form of nitroglycerin: dynamite (*see* page 52).

Nobel became wealthy from this discovery and his other invention, the sensitive blasting explosive gelignite, also called gelatin dynamite, a mixture of nitroglycerin and nitrocellulose. He was a pacifist who wanted his explosives used only for industrial purposes, and was upset when they were used in military weapons. After making a fortune, he set up the annual Nobel Prizes that have been awarded since 1901 for peace, physics, chemistry, physiology or medicine, and literature. Nobel died in 1896.

Alfred Nobel's accomplishments were more impressive because he spent only two terms in school and was in ill health for his entire life.

of this explosive. Armies had used gunpowder for some 500 years, but it exploded into thick smoke, obscured the battlefield, fouled cannons and small arms, and turned the gunners black. Schonbein's discovery could be used as a nearly "smokeless powder" to propel artillery shells. Schonbein studied in England under Michael Faraday (1791–1867) and also discovered **ozone** and manufactured the first cellulose nitrate plastics (*see* Chapter 1, page 18). Guncotton, however, was very unstable, and manufacturing it was dangerous—

some factories were blown up in the process. In 1844 or 1845, Italian chemist Ascanio Sobrero (1812–1888) discovered another unstable compound as he experimented with mixtures. When he combined nitric acid, sulfuric acid, and glycerol, the compound nearly exploded in his hands. He had created nitroglycerine, a mixture so unstable that it could be set off with the touch of a feather. Sobrero was later involved in a nitroglycerine explosion that left his face scarred. Later in life, he was quoted as saying: "When I think of all the victims killed during the nitroglycerine explosions and the terrible havoc that has been wreaked, which in all probability will continue to occur in the future, I am almost ashamed to admit to be its discoverer."

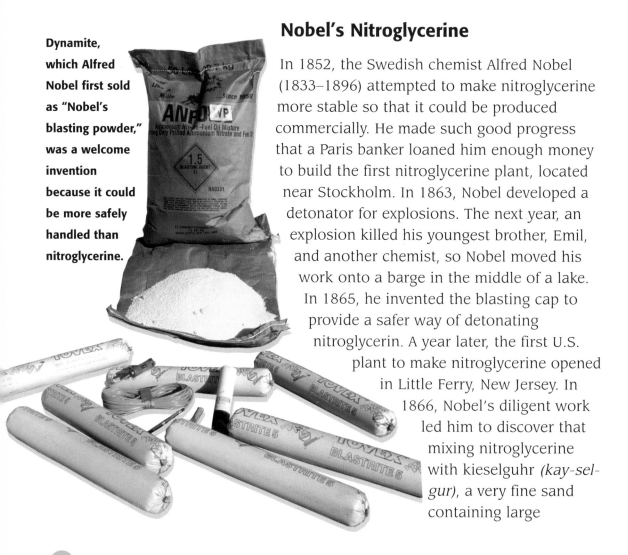

Dynamite, which Alfred Nobel first sold as "Nobel's blasting powder," was a welcome invention because it could be more safely handled than nitroglycerine.

Nobel's Nitroglycerine

In 1852, the Swedish chemist Alfred Nobel (1833–1896) attempted to make nitroglycerine more stable so that it could be produced commercially. He made such good progress that a Paris banker loaned him enough money to build the first nitroglycerine plant, located near Stockholm. In 1863, Nobel developed a detonator for explosions. The next year, an explosion killed his youngest brother, Emil, and another chemist, so Nobel moved his work onto a barge in the middle of a lake. In 1865, he invented the blasting cap to provide a safer way of detonating nitroglycerin. A year later, the first U.S. plant to make nitroglycerine opened in Little Ferry, New Jersey. In 1866, Nobel's diligent work led him to discover that mixing nitroglycerine with kieselguhr *(kay-sel-gur)*, a very fine sand containing large amounts of silica, produced a paste that could be rolled into rods that would explode only if detonated with a percussion cap. He had created the world's first safe high explosive, patenting it in 1867 under the name of dynamite, the Greek word for "power." In 1870, the first U.S. dynamite plant, the Giant Powder Company, opened in San Francisco. By the time the United States completed the Panama Canal in 1914, the greatest engineering project ever undertaken, construction workers had used 73 million pounds (33 million kilograms) of dynamite. In 1887, Nobel also invented and patented a smokeless propellant that he named ballistite. It was composed of nitroglycerin, collodion (nitrocellulose), and a small amount of camphor. This compound could become unstable after some time, because the camphor would often evaporate. Today, it is used as a solid rocket propellant.

In France in 1886, the chemist Paul Vieille (1854–1934) invented a smokeless powder called Poudre B (for Poudre Blanche, which means "white powder"). He took two forms of nitrocellulose (guncotton and collodion) and mixed them with **ethanol** and **ether**. This combination was three times as powerful as the old black powder and produced a clear explosion because it releases mostly gases instead of the solids released by black powder. Unfortunately, Poudre B became unstable with age. As a result, two of the French navy's battleships blew up in Toulon harbor—the *Jena* in 1907 and the *Liberté* in 1911.

In 1889, in Great Britain, the Scottish chemist James Dewar (1842–1923) and English chemist Frederick Augustus Abel (1827–1902) devised a safer compound. They mixed guncotton with nitroglycerin and a small amount of vaseline, using **acetone** as a solvent, to produce **cordite**—so called because it could be pressed into long spaghetti-like cords (it was first called "cord powder"). Cordite would be used in different mixtures through both world wars in firearms, artillery guns, and rockets. During World War II, **nitroguanidine** *(night-ro-gwan-i-dine)* was added to create Cordite N, which has a lower burning temperature than cordite, and causes less gun-barrel erosion.

TNT

The high explosive trinitrotoluene (TNT) was developed near the end of the nineteenth century (*see* Chapter 1, page 15). In fact, the German chemist Joseph Wilbrand (1811–1894) had discovered it in 1863, but nobody realized it could be

PROFILE **SIR JAMES DEWAR**

James Dewar was born in Kincardine-on-Forth in the Scottish county of Fife. He graduated from Edinburgh University and then taught chemistry at the Royal Veterinary College in Edinburgh, Cambridge University, and at the Royal Institution in London.

He devised the structure for benzene, a fuel accelerant, and joined with Sir Frederick Abel in the discovery of cordite (*see* page 53). Dewar built a device that produced liquid oxygen, which he used to experiment on meteorites. He also demonstrated that liquid oxygen and ozone are magnetic. His research was done at extremely low temperatures approaching absolute zero. At the Royal Institution, he built a giant refrigerating machine that liquefied hydrogen for the first time in 1898. To cool liquid gases, he surrounded them with a vacuum as insulation. This invention, the Dewar flask, later became a household item, the Thermos flask or pitcher. Dewar was knighted in 1904.

James Dewar's work earned him honors from the Smithsonian Institution, the Royal Society in Britain, the French Academy of Sciences, and other scientific organizations.

used as an explosive for another three decades. The German military began using it in 1902 and other countries soon followed. When World War I began, TNT became the most common explosive, and it continued to be the most widely used in World War II. It is relatively safe to handle because it is not affected by normal friction and shocks, and must be set off by a detonator. TNT does not absorb moisture, which is why it is used for underwater blasting,

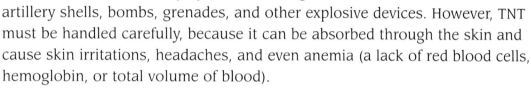

TATP, a white crystalline powder also known as acetone peroxide, was used by British terrorists who bombed London subway trains and a bus in 2005.

and it does not react with metals. TNT is a pale yellow crystalline solid made from the hydrocarbon **toluene** (now mostly from coal tar or petroleum) by adding it to sulfuric and nitric acids. It has a low melting point and can, therefore, be melted easily by steam heating to fill artillery shells, bombs, grenades, and other explosive devices. However, TNT must be handled carefully, because it can be absorbed through the skin and cause skin irritations, headaches, and even anemia (a lack of red blood cells, hemoglobin, or total volume of blood).

Liquid Explosives

Today's terrorists, including suicide bombers, often use new types of explosives. Although the German scientist Richard Wolffenstein discovered the liquid explosive triacetone triperoxide *(try-assa-tone try-per-oxide)* (TATP) in 1895, it was considered too unstable for use because of its sensitivity to friction and heat. In the early 1980s, however, terrorists began to prefer this so-called "Mother of Satan." On July 7, 2005, in London, it was used in the subway and bus bombings that killed fifty-two people and injured about 700. TATP was also intended as the trigger for the shoe-bomb that Richard Reid, a British subject, tried to explode on a flight from Paris to Miami in December 2001. It is commonly used by al-Qaeda and by Hamas suicide bombers who target Israel.

TATP's basic ingredients are easy to obtain without the buyer attracting any suspicion. This simple compound is almost impossible to detect, even by sniffer dogs and bomb-detection devices. The prime explosive in Reid's shoe bomb was pentaerythritol tetranitrate *(pen-ter-e-thry-tall tet-ra-night-rate)* (PETN), a high-grade plastic explosive—and, in fact, one of the strongest high explosives in existence. It belongs to the same chemical family as nitroglycerin. The military began to use it after World War I as an explosive in shells and landmines. It is mixed with TNT to form the explosive pentolite *(pen-tow-light)*.

Tool of the Terrorists

Liquid explosives are the latest terrorist threat and resulted in the near closure of British airports in August 2006 when a threat was suspected. U.S. Homeland Security Secretary Michael Chertoff said that there was a plot to blow up transatlantic airliners by terrorists who "planned to carry the components of the bombs, including liquid explosive ingredients and detonating devices, disguised as beverages, electronic devices, or other common objects." Other reports said the plotters would conceal their peroxide-based explosives in a sports drink and detonate it with a disposable camera's flash or by using heat or friction.

Liquid explosives are difficult to detect, because X-ray machines at airport security checkpoints cannot reliably tell the difference between regular beverages and liquid explosives. Of course, liquid explosives have long existed. Alfred Nobel first called nitroglycerin "blasting oil" before he mixed it with nitrocellulose into a glutinous substance he called "blasting gelatine."

In 1987, saboteurs apparently used a liquid explosive to blow up a Korean Air Lines flight. Passengers, believed to be North Korean agents, smuggled it on board in a bottle of alcohol and then got off the plane before the explosion that killed 115 people. In 1995, the terrorist Ramzi Yousef, who was involved in the 1993 bombing of the World Trade Center, was arrested in the Philippines two weeks before he planned to fill bottles of contact lens solution with nitroglycerin that would be connected to digital watches as timers, and batteries as a power source.

Kitchen-sink Explosives

Nitroglycerin is one of the liquid explosives easily available to bombmakers. A clear liquid explosive called Astrolite G can be produced by mixing ammonium nitrate with **hydrazine**, which is used to make rocket fuel. Astrolite G has an extremely high detonation velocity—it has been called "the world's most powerful non-nuclear explosive"—and is nearly twice as powerful as TNT. It has a low volatility, which means it can be spread over an area, be absorbed in the soil, and keep its full explosive power for about four days. Other dangerous liquids include the cleaning solvent nitromethane (*night-row-me-thane*) and also methyl nitrate, which is derived from nitric acid.

New explosives are always being developed. In 2000, researchers at the University of Chicago synthesized an explosive that could be made more powerful than any non-nuclear explosive. Their compound, octanitrocubane *(ock-tan-i-trock-u-bane)*, consists of carbon, nitrogen, and oxygen, with eight carbon atoms held at the corners of a cube in a crystal form. The Chicago scientists are now trying to increase the density of the crystalline form to create an even more powerful explosive.

KEY FACTS TYPES OF MILITARY EXPLOSIVES

All explosives are classified as primary or secondary. The former are also called initiating explosives because they are used to ignite the larger secondary ones that are the main charge. Military explosives are grouped by their usage:

• Propellants are low or burning explosives that launch rockets, torpedoes, bullets, and shells from guns.

• Bursting explosives are the high explosives used to damage a target being attacked. They are the destructive force in bombs, missiles, torpedo warheads, mines, and depth charges.

• Pyrotechnics are used for flares that send signals or illuminate an area, and for other jobs needing a good burning characteristic, such as tracers and smoke generators.

• Incendiaries have intense heat and flame so that they can start fires to damage materials and hurt personnel.

Bomb disposal experts detonate a land mine from a safe distance in Bosnia. Buried wartime mines continue to cause civilian injuries in several countries.

chapter 5

Detecting, Identifying, and Tracing Explosives

Investigators are quickly on the scene of an explosion, and any evidence they find is examined by specialist forensic scientists.

Gathering evidence after an explosion requires more intense work than it does for a fire investigation, because a blast will blow evidence over a large area. A 6,000-pound (2,700-kilogram) bomb, for instance, can spread evidence over 225 acres (91 hectares). Luckily for investigators, the explosion does not totally destroy the bomb or other device, so that they can begin an immediate search for the dispersed shrapnel. They can estimate the size of the bomb used by viewing the structural damage it caused—as was done very accurately when a bomb in a van destroyed the Federal Building in Oklahoma City on April 19, 1995. In the first hours after a large explosion, chaos and confusion reign. For this

◁ **Investigators in London, England, sift through debris after an explosion in 2005. Such painstaking work often recovers evidence that can be traced to its source.**

59

reason, the bombing site can be treated more like an accident scene than a crime scene. Items that are evidence of a crime may, at first, have to be ignored, because rescue workers have an extremely limited time to remove victims from the rubble. Even if evidence is discovered that indicates a criminal act, the removal of the injured and dead must take precedence over collecting the evidence.

Gathering Evidence

Investigators can determine the seat of the blast by the crater created, and the pressure of an explosion can create a unique scene. As a pressure wave rushes out from the point of detonation, it creates a vacuum behind it. When air rushes in to fill the vacuum, a wall will collapse back toward the seat of the explosion instead of outward.

In securing the scene, investigators place barriers beyond the area estimated to contain the thrown debris. Although television programs like *CSI*, *CSI: Miami* and *Bones* tend to glamorize forensic scientists' work, assignments at a bomb

The terrorist bombings in 2004 stunned the Spanish capital, Madrid. The explosions on commuter trains at rush hour killed 191 people, the country's deadliest terrorist attack.

scene can be very low tech. After the crater is searched for evidence, the larger area is divided into grid squares. Investigators then don rubber gloves and kneepads, form a line and crawl slowly over every inch, looking for chemical residues, and picking up debris with special tools to avoid contamination.

Even wood, soil, and furniture pieces should be collected, since they could hold residues of the explosive used. These dusty specimens are then carefully analyzed for fragments of the bomb, often using a fine wire screen to sift the debris. If tiny pieces are found, or even if no fragments are found, the blast was probably caused by a high explosive. In many cases, a surprising amount of a bomb's components—batteries, a clockwork mechanism, wires—are found. Sniffer dogs and devices that detect vapors help to locate explosives.

If the explosion was caused by a car bomb, the remains of the vehicle are securely covered by a tarpaulin and transported to a police garage for a lengthy examination. Much time is needed to investigate the scene, for a mere 10 pounds (4.5 kilogram) of explosives can scatter parts of a car 100 yards (92 meters) in every direction.

In the case of a bomb that has not exploded, a bomb squad should take photographs before detonating the device. This assists forensic scientists, though they would prefer a dismantled bomb to the remains of an exploded one.

As with fires, witnesses are important. In the Oklahoma City bombing, several eyewitnesses gave descriptions of the person who had rented the van. From these, a forensic artist drew a likeness that identified Timothy McVeigh, who was soon arrested.

Laboratory Testing

The recovered evidence is placed in new bags or containers, properly labeled, and carefully taken to a laboratory so that it does not become contaminated. In major bombings, the evidence usually involves several thousand items. At the lab, each piece receives a "Q" or "K" number. The "Q" stands for "Questioned," which is normally applied to pieces from the crime scene. The "K" indicates "Known," and would apply, for example, to a suspect's residence. The lab's forensic scientists first photograph each item, because tests during its examination could change its appearance. Chemists then search for microscopic particles of explosives on the debris, while **DNA** examiners process fragments

PROCEDURE **TRAINING SNIFFER DOGS**

Highly trained dogs, especially bloodhounds, can help identify bomb-makers and arsonists by recognizing scents left by the criminals. Some dogs can detect about 19,000 different combinations of explosives. Handlers train their dogs by letting them sniff a sample recovered from the crime scene, and then walking them in areas suspected of harboring the suspect.

In a recent test reported by the FBI Laboratory, six people handled four pipe bombs and two gas containers for one to two minutes. The items were then detonated or burned, and the debris collected and put onto surgical pads. These were kept from two to sixteen days before letting bloodhounds have a sniff. Because explosives are very volatile, the dogs are not allowed to touch the objects they sniff. They were then taken on trails in a city park, and the results were good. They correctly identified the target person in fifty-three of the eighty bomb experiments, and thirty-one of the forty arson ones. They made no false identifications.

President George W. Bush watches Robby, a sniffer dog, receive encouragement from his handler to inspect luggage for explosives in Beltsville, Maryland.

of bone, skin, and teeth to identify victims (including a suicide bomber).

The Bureau of Alcohol, Tobacco, Firearms and Explosives (ATF) Forensic Science Laboratory has investigated more explosions—including terrorist attacks such as the 1993 World Trade Center bombing—than any other lab in the world. The lab's staff members—explosive investigators and forensic chemists—work to identify the explosive used, the parts of the explosive device, and even marks caused by the tools used to build the bombs. When evidence arrives at the lab, experts examine it under a microscope to detect any traces of the explosive that have not been burned, and also to divide the different categories of evidence. When useful items are identified, they are washed in acetone or water because this absorbs explosives. They then run various tests. Thin-layer chromatography involves putting a solution along a coated plate that separates the different substances into spots. In liquid chromatography, a solution flows through a column of **adsorbent** that separates the different substances into bands or spots. In both versions, the results are displayed on a chromatograph that can be compared with the chromatograph for known explosives. Another test is gas chromatography with mass spectrometry (*see* Chapter 2, page 28).

A forensic scientist in Marseilles, France, examines evidence from fires in Lambesc and Calas in 2003. Included are cigarette ends, lighters, and a flammable cloth.

In 2004, at the University of Florida, a new detection technology was developed after the U.S. Army Research Office challenged universities to come up with a quick and reliable way to identify explosives. The university's method is based on **photoluminescence**. This directs a high-powered laser beam on

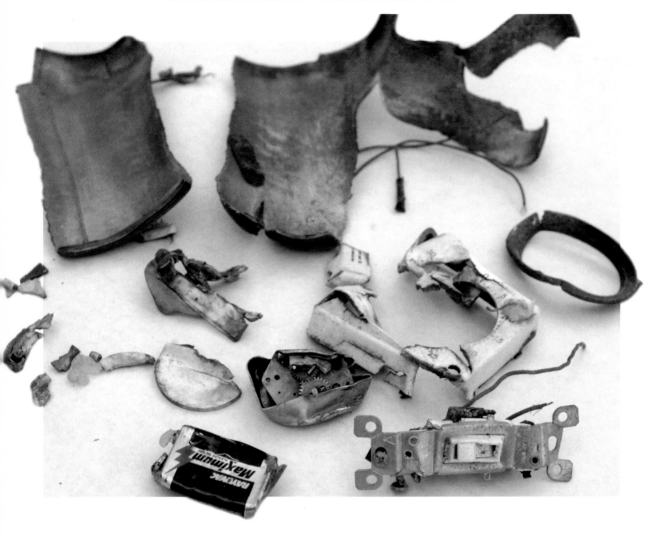

Debris from a pipe bomb is displayed November 17, 2003, at the Bureau of Alcohol, Tobacco, Firearms and Explosives (ATF) Fire Research Laboratory in Maryland.

an explosive's molecules, causing them to give off photons (light) that have the wavelength of a known material, such as TNT. Photoluminescence spectroscopy can get results from any contaminated item—from the surface of a suitcase to a speck of dust.

Worries about terrorism have intensified the search for even more powerful sensors to detect explosives such as homemade improvised explosive devices (IEDs). The National Science Foundation (NSF) requested $20 million from the federal government for 2007 in order to develop detectors with greater sensitivity and higher resolution. Research is already underway on an "electronic nose" that can duplicate the sensitivity of a dog's sensory system. Other ideas include miniaturized chemical analyzers and advances in tagging and tracing explosives. The NSF will work together with other branches of the federal government, such as the U.S. Navy, the Department of Defense, and the Department of Energy.

Telltale Signs

Recovered fragments of a bomb can yield substantial clues. Sometimes, a bomber's fingerprints survive an explosion. More likely to survive, though, are bomb parts that can be traced back to the manufacturer. The Explosive Unit of the Federal Bureau of Investigation (FBI) keeps an impressive collection of recovered bomb pieces and up-to-date examples of other bomb components, including detonators, batteries, switches, and wires. Laboratories with units specializing in explosives also hold large collections.

Future detection will dramatically improve if markers called **taggants** are introduced to commercially manufactured explosives. These microscopic pieces (about 1,000 **microns**) of multilayered colored plastic are added to the product in order to identify its source. When bomb pieces are recovered after a blast, their special taggant codes can be read by a lab microscope to find out who made them, as well as where and when. These markers can also be made to be fluorescent, so that they can be seen under ultraviolet light, as well as magnetic. The name comes from "Microtaggant Identification Particle," produced by the Microtrace company, which can create more than 37 million unique codes.

Although the Swiss government has adopted taggants for both high and low explosives, other countries have been slow to follow their example. Explosive manufacturers are worried about being sued when their products are involved in a crime, and in the United States, the powerful National Rifle Association (NRA) has resisted taggants in gunpowder, claiming that the devices would make the explosive unstable. Others dispute this.

Another type of marker is a glass microsphere, which is about the width of a human hair, and also contains a code that can trace the explosive back to the company, plant location, and even the day it was manufactured. Microspheres are already added to explosives to improve their performance.

KEY FACTS · THE FBI AND FORENSIC SCIENCE

July 1, 1924	The Bureau of Investigation (the FBI's original name) sets up an Identification Division with a fingerprint file.
November 24, 1932	The Bureau establishes a Technical Laboratory to provide services for federal, state, local, and foreign enforcement agencies.
August 31, 1940	The FBI establishes a Disaster Squad to investigate such tragedies as large explosions and air crashes.
January 1, 1967	The National Crime Information Center becomes operational. Law enforcement officials across the nation can tap into this electronic database.
April 3, 1978	The FBI Laboratory Division pioneers the use of laser technology to detect latent crime scene fingerprints.
1981	The FBI's Laboratory's Forensic Science Research and Training Center is established at the FBI Academy in Quantico, Virginia.
August 1991	The Computer Analysis and Response Team in the FBI Laboratory becomes operational to examine computers and computer disks during investigations.
July 1992	The FBI Laboratory installs DRUGFIRE, a database that stores and links unique markings left on bullets and shell casings.
1996	The Hazardous Materials Unit is established for incidents involving chemical, biological, and nuclear weapons.
December 8, 1997	The National DNA Index System allows forensic science labs to link violent serial crimes through the electronic exchange of DNA profiles.

Airport Security and Bomb Detection

The average person has become familiar with detection routines at airport security checkpoints. Checked and carry-on baggage, purses, coats, shoes, and other items are X-rayed by Explosive Detection System (EDS) machines that are about the size of a mini-van and are similar to a medical CAT scan. Screeners also use Explosive Trace Detection (ETD) machines that are about the size of a large suitcase. The latter involves using a swab on a piece of luggage, and analyzing the swab for traces of explosives.

When people check their bags at an airline counter, they are scanned by a simple X-ray machine. If anything seems suspicious, the luggage goes through a slower CT scanner, which surrounds the pieces with a rotating X-ray beam to produce a tomogram, a detailed cross-section. This can identify the density and mass of items inside. Carry-on luggage also goes through a machine that sends out X-rays with both high and low energy. The result is a color display of different items inside, with explosive powder showing as orange.

The technology of both scanners involves ion mobility spectrometry. When placed in an electric field, ions (charged molecules) move at different speeds, depending on their size and shape. Airport analyzers collect chemicals from luggage and other articles, place these chemicals in an electric field, and search for an ion that has the known speed of an explosive.

Passengers must also pass through a detector that resembles a doorframe. It sends out about 100 short pulses of current every second to create a magnetic field. If the pulses strike metal, they produce another magnetic field that slows the first one by a few

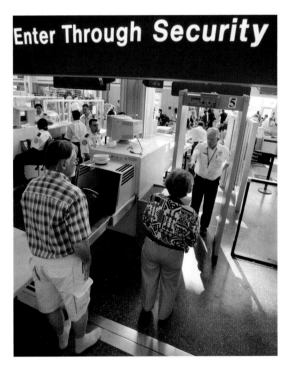

Passengers at the United Airlines terminal at Chicago's O'Hare Airport walk through X-ray machines after sending their carry-on bags for scanning.

microseconds, making the machine beep. The security official may then pass a wand around the passenger's body. This is an ETD screener with a dry pad at the end. The pad is then placed in an ion mobility spectrometer that can detect traces of explosives.

Unfortunately, a Homeland Security Department report says the X-ray machines are unable to detect liquid or gel explosives. This is one reason the Transportation Security Administration (TSA) banned liquids and gels on planes after British police foiled a terrorist plot to use them to blow up transatlantic flights in 2006. Most liquid explosives are made of unstable molecules. Nitroglycerin, oily and clear, is made of carbon, nitrogen, hydrogen, and oxygen. Any physical shock will start a chain reaction that breaks down the molecules to carbon dioxide, water, and oxygen, releasing a great amount of energy.

Some foiled attackers had intended to use triacetone triperoxide (*try-peh-rocks-eyed*), known as TATP, made from readily available hydrogen peroxide, acetone, and acid (*see* Chapter 4, page 55). Astrolite is another liquid explosive that comes in several different varieties. However, while all of these all require detonators, nitromethane, which is used to power model planes and rockets, only needs to be combined with another substance to explode.

TSA Anti-Terrorist Screening

Terrorists could bring dangerous liquids on board planes in bottles for products such as baby's formula, shampoo, lotion, perfume, or hair gel. Two different liquids might be mixed to start an explosion. One liquid could be dyed to look like a sports drink and then mixed with a peroxide. Cell phones or MP3 players might be used as detonators.

The latest explosive-trace detection machine, or "puffer" machine, releases several bursts of air at a passenger's body—face, torso, and legs—and analyzes the dislodged microscopic particles for any explosive residue. Passengers step into the machine, which is about 9 feet (3 meters) tall, and stand still for a few seconds. If a green light shines, no residue has been detected; if a red light shines, it means explosives are present. By August 2006, the TSA had installed the machines, at a cost of $160,000 each, in more than thirty airports nationwide. The TSA is testing biometric identification machines at airports and harbors across the country. These machines use scans of fingerprints and eyes

Police officers in Glasgow, Scotland, carefully monitor knives in a passenger's bag passing through an X-ray machine at Glasgow Airport.

Agents of the Transportation Security Administration (TSA) are in charge of security for U.S. airports, seaports, and the railroad system.

for identification purposes, to control access to important facilities. The iris, the colored part of the eye, has a unique pattern of markings for each eye, and these never change. The face is also used to identify people, using measurements between key points. When two or more biometric characteristics are used for identification, this is called a multimodal biometric system. The data is saved and stored in a chip, usually in a passport or ID card, and can be checked against future scans.

The TSA has also proposed a trial at several airports for "backscatter" X-ray machines that see through clothes, producing naked images of passengers. The machine uses low-energy X-rays to scan a person's form. Unlike a doctor's X-rays, which penetrate the body, these scatter and return to create an image, revealing hidden weapons or other objects. A passenger goes into a private area, lifts his arms, and faces three different directions. (To avoid embarrassment, the machine's operator is the same sex as the passenger.) The $200,000 machines have already been tried out at Orlando International Airport in Florida and Heathrow Airport in London, England.

New Detection Methods

Scientists continue to look for more efficient detectors. In 2006, the TSA began testing a ticketing machine to detect traces of explosives on the fingers of anyone buying a subway ticket in Baltimore. This early warning system has been developed by two companies, GE Security and Cubic Corporation.

At the University of Arizona, chemistry professors are developing a device that is 1,000 times more sensitive than equipment currently used in airports to detect explosives. It has the impressively long name of "capacitive transimpedance amplifer." Rather than using a swab on a briefcase, the new pocket-sized device is placed in a walk-through portal to detect traces of explosives in the air passing around a person who has handled explosives. The inventors say it is more sensitive than a dog's nose and can identify which explosive material is detected.

The ATF is the primary source of explosives investigation and training throughout the world. It starts and supports more criminal investigations into the unlawful use of explosives, and the manufacture and possession of IEDs than any other federal law enforcement agency. The agency recently added the

CASE STUDY THE *LOS ANGELES TIMES* BOMBING

A gigantic explosion woke up downtown Los Angeles just after 1:00 A.M. on October 1, 1910. The target was the *Los Angeles Times* building, which collapsed into rubble, killing twenty employees working on the next morning's edition. Soon after, two suitcases were found. One exploded, but no one was hurt.

Immediately on the case was detective William J. Burns (1860–1932). He examined the suitcase that had failed to explode and traced the dynamite type to its store, getting the names and descriptions of the buyers. The phony signatures were compared with handwriting on hotel registers and three men were identified. They were members of a union that had disputes with the newspaper. The famous lawyer Clarence Darrow defended the accused men but, seeing that Burns had too much evidence, they confessed the following year. Burns went on to uncover political corruption in San Francisco and become the director of the Bureau of Investigation (the FBI's former name) from 1921–1924. He trained a young assistant, J. Edgar Hoover, who would become the FBI's most famous director.

After the *Los Angeles Times* building was destroyed, the newspaper's owner, Harrison Gray Otis, found another bomb that exploded, but no one was hurt.

word "Explosives" to its title (but kept the acronym of ATF) when the 2002 Homeland Security Act transferred it from the Treasury to the Justice Department. The new name reflects its role in explosives regulation and enforcement. The Bureau also sets up arson and explosives task forces in cities and regions. On October 10, 2006, for example, it deputized all full-time bomb technicians of the Houston Police Department Bomb Squad as federal agents. This means that the Houston team can assist investigations throughout the United States, allowing leads to be pursued across local, state, and federal jurisdictions. A regional example is the Northern Virginia Arson and Explosives Task Force.

The ATF requires anyone selling explosives to have a license and user permit, and to submit fingerprints and photographs to the agency. It also circulates a list of the types of people not allowed to possess explosives, including non-citizens, anyone dishonorably discharged from the military, and those who have renounced their U.S. citizenship. In 2006, the ATF published a list of 238 explosive materials that are subject to regulation by federal law. These include explosives as well as blasting agents and detonators. Items on the list include dynamite, black powder, initiating explosives, igniters, and detonating cords.

The FBI and the Terrorist Screening Center

The FBI also leads in U.S. investigations and training on explosives, having a laboratory that handles more than one million examinations for bombings, arson, and other crimes. The FBI and the U.S. Army train the nation's 2,600 bomb technicians at their Hazardous Devices School at the Redstone Arsenal in Huntsville, Alabama. Since it opened in 1971, more than 7,500 members of bomb squads—firefighters, police officers, FBI agents, and other federal investigators— have completed the basic course.

The nation now has over 400 bomb squads. The school, which recently had a $25 million update, occupies a campus of nearly 300 acres (122 hectares), which includes fourteen mock villages, airline and bus terminals, homes, a strip mall, and a gas pipeline. The courses include: fundamentals of explosives; how to recognize, assess, and render hazardous devices safe; how to determine what exploded and why; fragment analysis; and even counterterrorism bomb training on how to respond to suicide attacks, large vehicle bombs, and weapons of mass destruction. The FBI has also sponsored more than seventy classes of these types around the nation, and two overseas. Backing up this detection system is the Terrorist Screening Center, a coordinated interagency effort administered by the FBI. This includes a Consolidated Terrorist Watchlist of the names and other identifying information for all known or suspected terrorists. The names are put on a Terrorist Screening Database, which is available to U.S. law enforcement agencies throughout the nation and also to some foreign governments.

In Canada, the Royal Canadian Mounted Police (RCMP) handles explosives incidents, doing the forensic investigation and tracing the explosive. Its Canadian Bomb Data Centre maintains a collection of information on explosives investigations, including product information, technical analysis of explosives, and case analysis. In 1993, it reported 317 incidents involving 1,074 explosive devices. The RCMP works with the Canadian Security Intelligence Service on terrorism. On June 2, 2006, members of the Royal Canadian Mounted Police and the Integrated National Security Enforcement Team arrested seventeen people trying to obtain three metric tons of ammonium nitrate and other components to create explosive devices. (The 1995 bombing that killed 168 people in Oklahoma City took only one metric ton.)

In the United Kingdom, bomb protection is the job of the Security Service, still commonly called MI5—Military Intelligence (Department) 5— although it was renamed in 1931. This agency investigates and traces all types of explosives, including incendiary, vehicle, and letter bombs, and incidents of suicide bombings. It is greatly helped by the London Metropolitan Police (Scotland Yard), which has officers who deal with all matters concerning explosives. It is

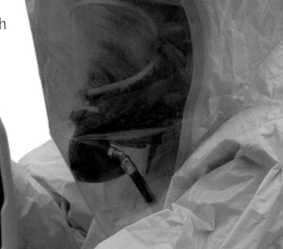

Spectrometers are used to identify explosives and other hazardous materials. This handheld instrument, FirstDefender, is produced by the Ahura Corporation of Wilmington, Massachusetts.

required that a person who receives or keeps explosives be licensed and that they keep accurate records of their stock. Britons who have criminal records are not allowed to handle or keep explosives. The Yard also has a Counter Terrorism Command.

In 2005, the European Union had plans to trace explosives by creating a European databank that could help track their sales and thefts.

PROFILE **DR. HENRY C. LEE**

One of the most famous forensic scientists in the world, Dr. Henry C. Lee, was born in China in 1938 and moved to New York in 1965 with his wife. He arrived with only $50 in his pocket. A former police captain in Taiwan, he received degrees from the John Jay College of Criminal Justice and New York University (NYU). He worked at NYU's Medical Center and then settled into the job of state police commissioner of Connecticut, establishing and becoming director of a modern police forensic science lab there, as well as professor of forensic science at the University of New Haven. In forty years, he has worked on more than 6,000 cases around the world, including the Jon Benet Ramsey murder case in Colorado.

"It's very important that everybody work together," he has said, "because the forensic field is a lonely and difficult field. You need everybody to push together." He also has tips for those interested in such a career. "You have to have a good science background. You need to have curiosity. You can't have an eight-to-four attitude."

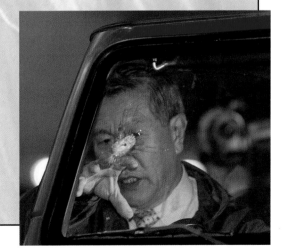

Dr. Lee (seen here examining a crime scene) was also involved in the forensic investigation after the 9/11 terrorist attacks, as well as the O. J. Simpson murder case.

chapter 6

Terrorism
and Explosives

More sophisticated detection methods are being used to discover explosives and track terrorists who pose a constant threat.

Although the United States and other governments are concerned about weapons of mass destruction, including chemical and biological agents, terrorists still almost always use bombs for their attacks. Bombs are fairly easy and cheap to make, and they are deadly.

The Bureau of Alcohol, Tobacco, Firearms and Explosives (ATF) teaches its bomb investigation techniques to the Army's explosives units before they are sent to Iraq, and also provides explosives training to the new Iraqi Police Service. Iraqi police investigate bomb scenes, gather intelligence about the devices that insurgents use and how they deploy them, and safely detonate unexploded bombs. The ATF's canine teams are now operating in Iraq and sixteen other foreign countries.

For its part, the Federal Bureau of Investigation (FBI) heads up the Terrorist Explosives Device Analytical Center (TEDAC), which was established in December 2003. The TEDAC's primary

◁ **An Iraqi policeman warns people to keep away from wreckage caused by a car bomb in the Baghdad shopping district of Karada.**

aim is providing a global response to terrorism, with a single federal program that collects intelligence on terrorist bombings and provides forensic analysis that is shared throughout the law enforcement, intelligence, and military communities.

The FBI keeps a fingerprint database in West Virginia, which contains approximately 50 million sets of prints. When the U.S. military recently rounded up suspected terrorists in Iraq, they took their fingerprints and sent them to the FBI through the Integrated Automated Fingerprint Identification System (IAFIS). Within just two hours, they could find out if any of the detainees had criminal histories in the United States—forty-four of them had. Local authorities also regularly use the database.

On September 15, 2006, when an explosion blew a hole in the window of Salt Lake City's main library, investigators found fingerprints on remnants of a hobby rocket igniter. The prints matched prints on file belonging to Thomas Zajac, who had previously been arrested in Ohio and Illinois. He was quickly arrested again. The Department of Defense has a similar biometric database of its own, the Automated Biometric Identification System (ABIS).

The Fly Team

The FBI's Fly Team is a highly trained group of agents and analysts who can be anywhere on the globe in just a few hours. Fly Team agents, who speak about a dozen languages, are bomb technicians, and experts on analyzing evidence and handling hazardous materials. They keep in contact with FBI headquarters through a secure computer network. In the last two years, the Fly Team has been called out on assignments more than seventy times, to Iraq, Afghanistan, Saudi Arabia, Turkey, Indonesia, and Morocco, among other destinations.

In today's war on terrorism, even information from a driver's license can be used for a full security check. A police officer making a traffic stop can check the information on the license against the FBI's National Crime Information Center (NCIC). If the query comes back with a warning flag from the Terrorist Screening Center (TSC), the officer then calls the TSC, which gives a link to the agency—for example, the FBI or CIA—that posted the original warning. The agency tells the officer how to proceed, including how to arrest the suspect. It all happens quickly.

The FBI's Fly Team went to Beirut, Lebanon, in 2005 to examine the car bomb that killed George Hawi, the former leader of the Lebanese Communist Party.

The method used to profile terrorists using explosives is more accurate than the method used for profiling arsonists. Terrorist bombers have a very different agenda, and their motives and backgrounds can often be placed within a narrow range. Gregg McCrary, who worked for twenty-five years as a profiler for the FBI, describes the process: "We start with an actual crime and crime scene, and then work backward to talk about the characteristics and traits of the particular individual who might have done that crime."

Oklahoma City Bombing

America's worst home-grown terrorist incident was the truck bomb attack on the Alfred P. Murrah Federal Building in Oklahoma City, on April 19, 1995, which killed 168 people, including nineteen children, and injured 850 more. The ATF and FBI formed the OKBOBMB Task Force, which was made up of fifty-six field officers. Agents

The Oklahoma City bombing was the worst terrorist attack on U.S. soil before September 11, 2001, and the worst ever by a U.S. citizen.

collected 23,290 items of evidence, including the truck's rear axle. Even though the axle had been thrown some distance, its serial number was intact. They also found the rear bumper with the license plate number. Both were traced to a Ryder rental agency in Junction City, Texas. The owner and employees were able to describe the customer, who had used the alias Robert King. A local motel manager recognized a police sketch as a man who had checked in under his real name of Timothy McVeigh.

The suspect was already in jail, having been arrested in his getaway car for driving without a license plate. The evidence mounted as an FBI chemist discovered traces of the fertilizer-based explosive on McVeigh's clothing. Another FBI forensic scientist found his fingerprints on a receipt for the materials used to make the bomb. McVeigh was found guilty and executed by lethal injection, while his accomplice, Terry Nichols, was sentenced to life.

In 2003, the FBI foiled another similar attack. The convict Gale Nettles, who was about to be released from prison in Mississippi, planned to blow up the federal courthouse in Chicago with a fertilizer-based explosive more powerful than McVeigh's. Nettles made the mistake of confiding in a fellow prisoner, who contacted police. The FBI had this prisoner arrange for Nettles to meet someone who would provide him with ammonium nitrate. This was a sting operation: the seller was an FBI agent who sold Nettles 2,000 pounds (907 kilograms) of a harmless fertilizer. Nettles then decided he could sell some for profit, so he asked the secret agent to introduce him to someone in al-Qaeda. Another agent posed as a terrorist, paying him $10,000 for the fertilizer. Nettles was arrested a short time later and given a life sentence.

The FBI Abroad

The FBI also conducts extensive investigations in foreign countries. Its largest ever investigation on foreign soil followed the U.S. embassy bombings on August 7, 1998, in Tanzania and Kenya that killed 227 people, including twelve Americans, and wounded more than 5,000.

Working with authorities from those two countries, FBI agents were able to trace the terrorists who had bought the truck used to carry the Tanzania bomb and to obtain records proving that they purchased the oxygen and acetylene tanks used in the detonation. By the time of the trial in New York, the agents

PROFILE TIMOTHY McVEIGH

The infamous Oklahoma City bomber was born on April 23, 1968, in Pendleton, New York, near Buffalo. His parents divorced in 1986, and he lived with his father, who was a very devout Roman Catholic. The young McVeigh joined the U.S. Army in 1988 and served in the Persian Gulf War in 1991, earning the Bronze Star. After the war, he tried to become a Green Beret but failed because of his lack of physical fitness. McVeigh left the army that year to work as a security guard near his hometown of Pendleton. In 1993, he began to attend gun shows around the United States. That same year, he was an onlooker at the ATF and FBI siege of the Branch Davidian religious cult center in Waco, Texas, where four agents and eighty-two cult members were killed. McVeigh wanted revenge for this federal action. In 1994, new laws restricting the purchase of certain types of guns further fuelled his anger. The following year, he bombed the federal building in Oklahoma City on April 19—the anniversary of the Waco incident.

Timothy McVeigh's planned escape went awry when he was arrested 90 minutes after the bombing for driving without a license plate.

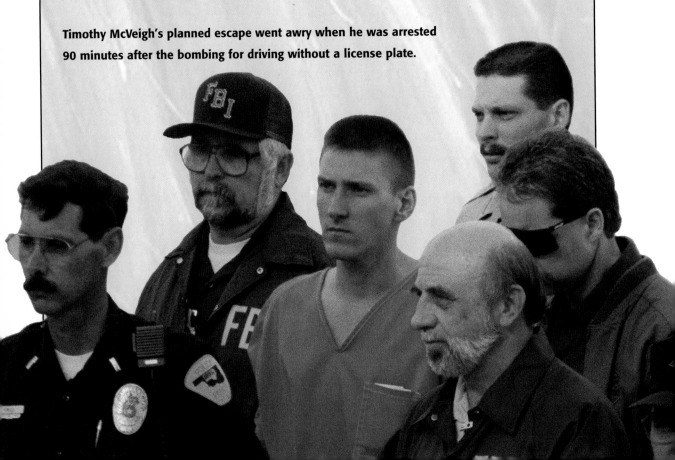

had helped to round up defendants and witnesses from three continents and produced more than 50,000 pages of exhibits. Three of the four terrorists confessed, and all were given life sentences without the possibility of parole.

One of the most complicated forensic investigations followed the bombing on December 21, 1988, of Pan American Flight 103 over Lockerbie, Scotland, killing 270 people (all the crew and passengers and eleven from the village below). It was the worst ever act of terrorism against a U.S. airline. More than 1,000 police and soldiers searched 845 square miles (2,189 square kilometers) of the Scottish countryside and found more than 10,000 pieces of evidence. Spy satellites also took high-resolution photographs of the site. Forensic scientists began their work and, according to the New York Times, "Their forensic wizardry would leave Sherlock Holmes shaking his head in wonder."

Just a week after the crash, investigators found traces of the plastic high explosive Semtex-H and even identified the two blackened suitcases that had held it. The explosive was traced to the Czech village that had manufactured it, and records showed that some of the explosive had been sold to the Libyan government. FBI agents helped identify another item found, a fragment of a circuit board timer similar to one previously seized from a Libyan intelligence agent. The remains of a baby's romper suit, adult clothes (one T-shirt with a label saying "Made in Malta"), and an umbrella were identified as wrappings for the bomb. They were traced to the Yorkie Clothing Company on the island of Malta and then to Mary's House, a clothing shop. The owner identified the buyer as a Libyan named Abdel Baset Ali Mohmed Al-Megrahi, who was with another Libyan. The men were not handed over for trial by Libya until 1999. In 2001, Megrahi was found guilty and sentenced to life in prison in Glasgow, Scotland. His supposed accomplice was found not guilty.

Attacks Against Airlines

Terrorist attacks on airlines seem a relatively modern crime, but the first recorded bombing of a commercial aircraft was in 1949, when an in-flight explosion killed all thirteen people aboard a Philippine Airlines DC-3. A woman was convicted of placing a bomb on the flight to kill her husband.

The first case solved with the help of forensic scientists was in Canada. On September 9, 1949, a bomb exploded on board a Canadian Pacific Airlines DC-3 en route from Montreal to Baie-Comeau, killing all nineteen passengers, including four children, and the four crewmembers. Albert Guayhad arranged for the bomb to be put on board during a stopover at L'Ancienne-Lorette, a suburb of Quebec City. He wanted to kill his wife so that he could live with his mistress. He had a clockmaker manufacture a bomb using dynamite, batteries, and an alarm clock. His mistress's sister bought the dynamite and delivered the bomb. During the investigation, Montreal's Laboratory of Forensic Medicine and Science identified the explosives using an emission spectrograph, which records spectra on a photographic plate. Witnesses had already identified the sister, Marguerite Ruest-Pitre. She, Guay, and his mistress, were convicted and hanged. Marguerite was the last woman in Canada to be executed in this manner.

In 1985, terrorists caused Canada's largest mass murder, when 329 people, including eighty-two children, died in the bombing of Air India Flight 182 as it approached the coast of Ireland. The victims included 280 Canadian citizens, most of them born in India or of Indian descent. The investigation was the longest, most complicated, and expensive in Canadian history, estimated at some 130 million Canadian dollars (112 million US dollars). The investigation found that two pieces of luggage had been checked in at Vancouver International Airport. One exploded at the baggage terminal at Tokyo's Narita Airport while being transferred to the doomed flight. The other brought down the plane. Pieces of the bomb in Tokyo were recovered and investigators matched these with items, including a stereo tuner that housed the bomb, that Inderjit Singh Reyat had purchased. Reyat, a British citizen, was found guilty of manslaughter in 1991 and served ten years in prison. The trial of other suspects supposedly behind the bombing collapsed for lack of evidence, even though investigators had spent fifteen years gathering it. In 2003, on his release, Reyat pleaded guilty to aiding in the construction of the bomb on the aircraft and was sentenced to five more years.

The Madrid Bombing

Spain's worst terrorist attack, the Madrid train bombings, took place on March 11, 2004. The attack killed 191 and injured 1,755. However, investigators found forensic evidence that led to an extensive roundup of suspects. Ten backpack bombs exploded during the morning rush hour and three failed to go off. Mobile

The front of Pan American's Boeing 747 on the crash site in the Scottish countryside after a terrorist bomb killed all on board on December 21, 1988.

phones used as detonators were traced to a Moroccan merchant, while the plastic explosives used were linked to a retired miner who still had access to blasting equipment.

Although the Spanish government said the attack was by the country's ETA separatist group, forensic analysis suggested otherwise. One of the unexploded devices was not like ETA's typical dynamite bombs; it was instead made of high-explosive Goma-2, a gelatinous nitroglycol *(night-row-gliss-all)* explosive, similar to nitroglycerine, but more volatile. Investigators also collected phone records and financial statements. Seven bombing suspects committed suicide during police raids. The trial of twenty-nine suspects—five charged with the killings and the others as accomplices—began in early 2007.

The Unabomber

Some explosion investigations go on for years without results. Then, sometimes, investigators get a lucky break. This happened to the authorities trying to track

A member of the Royal Canadian Mounted Police guards the wreckage of Air India Flight 182, which was bombed on June 23, 1985, killing all on board.

down the "Unabomber," who sent sixteen bombs to universities and airlines from 1978 to 1995, killing three and wounding twenty-nine others. The name came from the FBI's nickname for the case, UNABOM, for "university and airline bomber." Despite the federal agencies' advanced forensic-science technology and their large task force, the Unabomber escaped capture for eighteen years, making this the longest and costliest manhunt for a serial murderer in U.S. history.

In that period, the FBI, the ATF, U.S. postal inspectors, and others received approximately 20,000 telephone tips, conducted thousands of interviews, drew up a list of more than 200 suspects, and even checked the names of people who withdrew certain library books. The pieces of the exploded bombs provided no evidence, since the Unabomber scraped off battery serial numbers and used wires no longer in production.

The break came only after the killer promised to stop the bombings if the *New York Times* and *Washington Post* would print his 35,000-word manifesto about the dangers of modern technology. On reading it, David Kaczynski noted it contained wording similar to some of his brother's writing, which he had found while cleaning out his mother's attic. He informed the FBI, and they tracked down the Harvard-educated, former math professor Theodore "Ted" Kaczynski to his hermit's cabin near Lincoln, Montana. He pleaded guilty and is now serving a life sentence without the possibility of parole.

CASE STUDY THE "SHOE BOMBER"

Richard Reid of London tried to board a plane to Miami on December 21, 2001, but he raised suspicions, paying for his ticket in cash and having no luggage to check in. Airport security questioned him for so long that he missed the flight. The next day, however, he was on American Airlines Flight 63 to Miami, preparing to blow it from the skies.

Reid was born August 12, 1973, in the London suburb of Bromley. His mother was English and his father Jamaican. They divorced when he was sixteen. Young Richard served several jail sentences, the first for mugging a senior citizen. While in prison, he converted to Islam, taking the name of Abdel Rahim. He later spent time in Pakistan and, possibly, Afghanistan.

His terrorist attack was foiled when a flight attendant saw him trying to light a match. When warned that smoking was not allowed, he promised to stop. Soon, however, she saw him holding a lit match and, in his lap, a shoe with a fuse. She grabbed him but he shoved her to the floor. Another flight attendant and some passengers finally subdued Reid, who was then handcuffed. Officials found pentaerythritol tetranitrate plastic explosives with an organic peroxide explosive (TATP) detonator in the lining of his shoes (*see* Chapter 4, page 55). He was found guilty of terrorism in 2003 in federal court in Boston, Massachusetts, and is serving a life sentence.

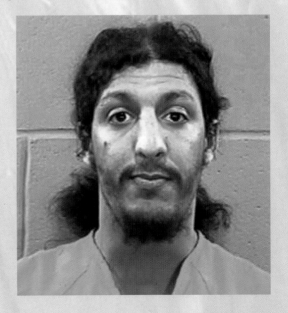

Before his attempted airline bombing, Richard Reid is believed to have traveled to Pakistan, Afghanistan, and several other countries harboring terrorists.

Another frustrating investigation happened after an explosion during the Atlanta Olympics in 1996. Three pipe bombs tied together went off in Centennial Olympic Park, killing one person and seriously injuring more than 100 others. One newsman also had a heart attack and died. The ATF and the FBI formed the Southeast Bomb Task Force, and worked closely together on the case, recovering smokeless powder used in the 12-inch (30-centimeter) pipes, as well as pieces of the bomb and nails inside it. They traced the 12-volt battery by its lot number to a chain of Florida hardware stores. Unfortunately, the customer who bought it could not be identified.

Before he became the terrorist known as the "Unabomber," Theodore Kaczynski was a brilliant student and professor.

In 1997, similar bombs exploded in Atlanta at a gay nightclub and at an abortion clinic. In 1998, there were further explosions at an abortion clinic in Birmingham, Alabama. In the latter case, a police officer was killed and bystanders wrote down the license plate number of a pickup truck owned by Eric Rudolph. He was later spotted near the Nantahala National Forest in North Carolina, which began a multimillion-dollar manhunt involving hundreds of officers. However, Rudolph evaded them in the 500,000-acre (202,500-hectare) forest for five years, and was captured only when a local police officer arrested him as a burglary suspect. He confessed to all the bombings and received consecutive six life sentences plus 120 years. He also disclosed three areas in North Carolina where 150 pounds (68 kilograms) of dynamite were buried, including a fully constructed dynamite bomb with a detached detonator. These were found and removed by a "render-safe" team of FBI and ATF explosives experts.

CCTV Evidence

One device used more and more by investigators, especially in Britain, is the closed circuit television (CCTV) camera. An array of these public surveillance cameras played the key role in identifying the four suicide bombers who, on July 7, 2005, attacked three trains on the London Underground and a double-decker bus, killing fifty-two people and themselves, and injuring more than 700 others. Investigators looked at approximately 2,500 pieces of CCTV footage and saw the bombers walking through a station with their backpacks. At the same time, forensic scientists examined remnants of the bombs that proved to be 10 pounds (4.5 kilograms) of a high explosive, acetone peroxide. The terrorists had also carried items of identification that were later recovered, leading investigators to a bomb factory in the city of Leeds, northern England. One bomber's car was found at a railroad station and still contained explosives. These identifications have led to an expanded search and the surveillance of others who might have been connected with the crime.

Forensic scientists are often the decisive witnesses in court cases involving explosions and fire. For this reason, it is important that they remain neutral. During one trial in England of an IRA terrorist suspect, the court noted: "For lawyers, jurors, and judges, a forensic scientist conjures up the image of a man

in a white coat working in a laboratory, approaching his task with cold neutrality, and dedicated only to the pursuit of scientific truth. It is a somber thought that the reality is sometimes different. Forensic scientists may become partisan. The very fact that the police seek their assistance may create a relationship between the police and the forensic scientists."

Fortunately for the justice system, the vast majority of these public servants are impartial and "dedicated only to the pursuit of scientific truth," to make the world safer from arsonists, bombers, and other criminals. As Dr. Henry C. Lee, the famed forensic scientist, noted: "Win, lose, or draw, you don't care. Don't let public opinion pressure you. Don't let the police pressure you. Don't let anything pressure you to do something unethical. Then you can survive and become one of the best forensic scientists."

◁ **Investigators search the area around a double-decker bus bombed in London on July 7, 2005.**

▷ **The TSA employs some 50,000 people. In March 2003, the organization was moved from the Department of Transportation to the Department of Homeland Security.**

KEY FACTS   THE TSA

The Transportation Security Administration (TSA) was created in response to the terrorist attacks on the United States on September 11, 2001. The TSA was established eight days later, when President George W. Bush signed the Aviation and Transportation Security Act. This made security for civil aviation a direct federal responsibility for the first time in U.S. history.

On February 17, 2002, the TSA took over security in the nation's 450 commercial airports from the Federal Aviation Administration (FAA) and the duty of baggage screening from private companies. This was the largest civilian undertaking in the history of the U.S. government.

To most travelers, airport screening checkpoints are their clearest look at the TSA, but the agency also keeps a Secure Flight and Registered Traveler list in order to find anyone who may pose a threat. The Secure Flight section collects information on passengers from airlines and checks it against a watchlist maintained by the Terrorist Screening Center, an interagency administered by the FBI (*see* Chapter 5, page 73). The Registered Traveler program provides quicker screening for passengers who have volunteered biometric and biographic information. The TSA's "No-Fly" list bans those on the list from flying. The agency also oversees the federal air marshals, who take flights as plainclothes police. In 2006, the TSA had 425 canine teams searching seventy-five airports for explosives in aircraft, luggage, cargo, terminals, vehicles, and warehouses. It also controls security for railroad, bus, and ferry systems.

Glossary

accelerants fuels used to start or intensify a fire, such as gasoline

acetone a volatile, flammable liquid substance used mainly in solvents

adsorbent a solid substance (usually) that absorbs thin layers of gases or liquids that it comes into contact with

alchemist a person who studies or practices alchemy, a medieval speculative science devoted to turning base metals into gold, discovering a cure for all diseases, and a way to prolong life

ammonium nitrate a colorless, crystalline salt used in explosives, as fertilizer, and in veterinary medicine

arson the act of unlawfully setting a fire, to damage property or cover up another crime

Astrolite G a liquid explosive made by mixing ammonium nitrate with anhydrous hydrazine

brisant explosive an explosive that creates a shock wave and shatters objects; also called a bursting explosive

calibrate to adjust something precisely so that it can carry out a particular function

chaparral dense thickets of shrubs and small trees; also shrubby plants that flourish in dry summers and moist winters such as occur in southern California

char the mostly carbon leftover of a material after it has been burned

cordite a smokeless explosive made of nitroglycerine, guncotton, petroleum jelly, and acetone

DNA deoxyribonucleic (dee-oxy-ry-bo-nu-kle-ik) acid; the substance found in the cells of living things that contain the genes, which control heredity

detonator a small primary charge used to set off a secondary charge

ethanol a colorless, volatile, flammable liquid that is present in alcoholic drinks and is used in solvents

ether a light, volatile, flammable liquid used mainly in solvents

firebreak a barrier of clear or plowed land intended to stop the progress of a fire

fire triangle the essentials needed to produce fire: heat, fuel, and oxygen

fire whirls tornado-like winds created by fires

friction the rubbing together of two objects to create a spark or flame

fuel load an amount of combustible material around a fire

gas chromatography a process that separates a solution or gas into various distinct bands or spots that are displayed on a chromatograph

Greek fire a weapon employed by the ancient Greeks, consisting of a liquid petroleum; it was also called "wild fire"

gunpowder black powder made by mixing oxidizers and fuels; it was commonly used for hundreds of years but produced thick black smoke

halogenated compounds substances treated or combined with any of the following five elements: fluorine, chlorine, bromine, iodine, and astatine

homicide murder

hydrated alumina aluminum oxide containing water—for example, bauxite

hydrazine a colorless, smoking liquid base used in fuels for rockets and jet engines

hydrocarbon an organic compound (for example, acetylene or butane) containing carbon and hydrogen, and often found in petroleum, natural gas, and coal

mass spectrometry a method that uses special instruments to identify the chemicals that make up a substance

micron a one-millionth part of something

nitroglycerine an unstable explosive oil used for making dynamite

nitroguanidine a stable explosive powder

nuclei plural of nucleus, the positively charged portion of an atom that contains most of the atom's mass and consists of protons and neutrons, except in hydrogen, which consists of only one proton

oxidizers an agent that combines a substance with oxygen

ozone a bluish, strong-smelling gas that occurs naturally as a pollutant in the lower atmosphere, and beneficially in the upper atmosphere

photoluminescence the emission of light that is caused by electromagnetic radiation falling on matter; a simple form would have a photon absorbed and an equivalent one emitted immediately

propellants types of low-burning explosives that launch rockets, torpedoes, bullets, and shells

pyrotechnics fireworks used for entertainment or as flares for signaling

solvent a liquid used to dissolve other substances

subsonic relating to speeds less than the speed of sound in air

taggants microscopic pieces of multilayered colored plastic added to a product to identify its source

TATP the organic peroxide explosive, often used by terrorists

toluene a liquid hydrocarbon, similar to benzene but less volatile

ultraviolet light light beyond the visible spectrum at its violet end, with wavelengths shorter than those of visible light and longer than those of X-rays

vacuum a space that contains absolutely nothing

vital reactions reactions that show whether or not a person was still alive at the moment of injury

Learn More About

A wealth of information on fire and explosives, as well as a broader look at forensic science, is available from the various media. Listed below are books and Web sites that link to government bureaus, professional bodies, reports, magazine and newspaper articles, and other sources.

Books

Ackerman, Thomas. *FBI Careers*. Indianapolis, Indiana: Jist Works, 2005.

Angle, James A. *Firefighting Strategies and Tactics*. Albany, New York: Delmar Learning, 2001.

Bouguard, Thomas J. *Arson Investigation: The Step-by-Step Procedure*. Springfield, Illinois: Charles C. Thomas Publisher, 2004.

Camenson, Blythe. *Opportunities in Forensic Science Careers*. New York: McGraw-Hill Publishing, 2001.

Ford, Jean Otto. *Explosives and Arson Investigation*. Broomall, Pennsylvania: Mason Crest Publishers, 2005.

George, Charles and Linda George. *Bomb Detection Dogs*. Mankato, Minnesota: Capstone Press, 1998.

Pickett, Mike. *Explosives Identification Guide*. Albany, New York: Delmar Learning, 2004.

Souter, Janet. *Air Marshal and Careers in Transportation Security*. Berkeley Heights, New Jersey: Enslow Publishers, 2006.

White, Jonathan R. *Terrorism and Homeland Security*. Belmont, California: Wadsworth Publishing, 2005.

Wright, John. *The U.S. Transportation Security Administration*. Broomall, Pennsylvania: Mason Crest Publishers, 2003.

Web Sites

American Academy for Forensic Sciences (AAFS): www.aafs.org

Alcohol, Tobacco, Firearms and Explosives (ATF): www.atf.treas.gov

Arson dogs: http://library.thinkquest.org/CR0210580/arsondog.htm

ATF for kids: www.atf.gov/kids

Central Intelligence Agency (CIA): www.cia.gov

CIA for kids: www.cia.gov/cia/ciakids/govagency.shtml

Explosive classifications: http://www.ordnance.org/

Federal Bureau of Investigation (FBI): www.fbi.gov

FBI for kids: www.fbi.gov/fbikids.htm

FBI laboratory: www.fbi.gov/hq/lab/labhome.htm

National Fire Protection Association: www.nfpa.org

National Interagency Fire Center: www.nifc.gov

Royal Canadian Mounted Police: www.rcmp-grc.gc.ca

Transportation Security Administration (TSA): www.tsa.gov

About the Author

John D. Wright is an American author and editor living in England. He has been a reporter for *Time* and *People* magazines, covering such subjects as politics, crime, and social welfare. He has also worked as a journalist for the U.S. Navy and for newspapers in Alabama and Tennessee. In 2002, he contributed to the *Crime and Detection* series for Mason Crest Publishers. He holds a Ph.D. degree in Communications from the University of Texas and has taught journalism in three universities.

Quoted Sources

p. 26—Dr. Henry C. Lee interviewed on Court TV's Crime Library at
www.crimelibrary.com/criminal_mind/forensics/lee/4.html

pp. 29–30—Greg Ecklund, WLTB 3, Jackson, Mississippi, at www.wlbt.com

p. 31—WLBT 3, Jackson, Mississippi, May 1, 2004
www.wlbt.net/Global/story.asp?S=1831788&nav=2csf

p. 35—*Fire Lover: A True Story* (2002) by Joseph Wambaugh

p. 36—From the FBI study, "The Firesetter: A Psychological Profile"; quoted in *New York Times*, December 7, 2006

p. 38—Dr. Alan Feldberg, Cornell Abraxas Group, Pennyslvania—The WebMD
www.webmd.com/content/article/76/90030.htm

p. 52—Nobel Prize biography
http://nobelprize.org/alfred_nobel/biographical/articles/life-work/sobrero.html

p. 56—Radio Free Europe August 10, 2006; "Government Executive" magazine,
www.govexec.com/dailyfed/0806/081006j1.htm

p. 75—"Forensic Science Education," Court TV Crime Library
www.crimelibrary.com/criminal_mind/forensics/lee/4.html

p. 80—Gregg McCrary interviewed on Court TV's Crime Library at
www.crimelibrary.com/crimina_mind/profiling/mccrary/3.html

p. 83—*New York Times*, April 29, 1990

p. 89—"Report on the Prevention of Miscarriage of Justice," (Canadian government), September 2004

p. 90—Dr. Henry C. Lee interviewed on Court TV's Crime Library at
www.crimelibrary.com/criminal_mind/forensics/lee/4.html

Index

Page numbers in *italics* refer to photographs.